A Skilfully Woven Knot

A Skilfully Woven Knot

Anglican Identity and Spirituality

Michael Mayne

Edited, with an Introduction,
by
Joel W. Huffstetler

CANTERBURY
PRESS
Norwich

© The estate of Michael Mayne, 2019

Introduction © Joel W. Huffstetler, 2019

First published in 2019 by the Canterbury Press Norwich

Editorial office

3rd Floor, Invicta House

108–114 Golden Lane

London EC1Y 0TG, UK

www.canterburypress.co.uk

Canterbury Press is an imprint of Hymns Ancient & Modern Ltd (a registered charity)

Hymns Ancient & Modern® is a registered trademark of Hymns Ancient & Modern Ltd

13A Hellesdon Park Road, Norwich,

Norfolk NR6 5DR, UK

British Library Cataloguing in Publication data

A catalogue record for this book is available

from the British Library

978 1-78622-132-2

Printed and bound in Great Britain by CPI Group (UK) Ltd

Contents

To Betty and Ben Calloway

Acknowledgements

Thanks to Alison Mayne for her support of, and help with, this project, and for our friendship. And thanks to Debbie Huffstetler, who has been involved with this project at every stage, including typing the manuscript. Thank you, my love.

All royalties from the sale of this book are donated to Book Trust UK in honour of Alison Mayne and in memory of Michael Mayne.

Joel Huffstetler

Foreword

JEFFREY JOHN

Michael Mayne embodied a gentle, cultured, liberal Anglicanism that is harder to find now. In the address that gives this collection its title, he presents it as a version of Christian faith marked, in words borrowed from Will Hutton, by 'inclusiveness, kindness and tolerance'. As an historian, Mayne understood that Anglican comprehensiveness is a hard-won thing, the product of years of bloody doctrinal and political conflict. As a theologian, he also knew that our view of Truth is always partial, and that we need one another's different views to enlarge our own vision. In his sermon 'On a Huge Hill' he quotes Donne:

> On a huge hill
> Craggy and steep, Truth stands, and he who will
> Seek him about must, and about must go.

Mayne insisted, in face of the growing polarization of the Church, that Anglican comprehensiveness is a strength, not a weakness; and although his own liberal inclinations were clear, he wanted all views heard and included. Had he lived longer, he would certainly have embraced 'good disagreement' as a truly Anglican policy. Occasionally one would like to press him harder, as one would like to press archbishops, on the limits of comprehensiveness, and in particular on the realism and cost of tolerating the constitutionally intolerant. How can the nest include the cuckoo and the brood still survive? He knew the paradox; but his determination that the Church must embrace all, because God's love embraces all, never wavered.

Just prior to his time as Dean of Westminster, Mayne's deep confidence in the love of God was tested, refined and deepened in the fire of a long illness. When he was struck down by ME the disease had barely been researched, and even some doctors were dismissing it as 'yuppie flu'. He painfully described the physical battle with neuralgia and total exhaustion, and the psycho-spiritual battle with loneliness, prayerlessness and the sense of rejection, in his book *A Year Lost and Found*. This book has helped many others get through similar struggles, but it still earned him the contempt of some, like the aged priest mentioned in 'The Other Side of the Dark', who asked him, 'Do you like to undress in public?'

Being able to share the experience of pain at least gave it a purpose. Mayne recalls that when he was asked, in the middle of his illness, what he *really* wanted in his deepest self, he realized it was above all to see some point in it, and so to redeem it. A second gain was a deeper grasp of the meaning of the cross for our own experience. For anyone who suffers, the most important thing to see is that God is not far away, deciding who suffers and who does not, but that God is vulnerable too and goes through it with us. Mayne's favourite quotation was one of John Austin Baker's: 'The crucified Jesus is the only accurate picture of God the world has ever seen.'

Some of his most striking reflections are on theology and art. Art operates independently of religion to give us insights into God's reality in the world, and at a time when the Church is widely rejected we need art to keep alive the perception of God, and simultaneously the perception of what it means to be human. Mayne describes the motivating factor of his life as the search for authenticity, by which he means the ultimate values of truth, beauty and goodness, which he finds in the greatest art as well as in worship. Having an aesthetic perception is therefore as vital as having an ethical one, and furthermore (a lovely observation, this) God enjoys the products of our creating too:

> I like to think that God has placed us on earth not to judge us, but to enjoy us, to enjoy not least our creativity, and that our obligations to him are no less aesthetic than moral.

Art keeps humanity human by allowing even those of us who think they are unreligious to glimpse the divine in themselves. But the royal way that unites us with God remains the Church's daily round of worship, the *Opus Dei*. For Mayne, as for St Benedict, nothing matters more, because worship not only glorifies God, it also heightens and activates his image in us:

> Once you dismiss the mystery of each human being made in the divine image; once awe and wonder count for nothing; once our sense of the holy and transcendent is denied, then life becomes cheap and it becomes possible to shatter with a single bullet those most miraculous objects, the human brain and the human heart, with scarcely a second thought. By our daily round of prayer and worship, the doing of the *Opus Dei*, we stand with those who affirm night and day that God is worthy of our love and praise, and that every living soul, made in God's likeness, is of infinite value in his sight.

That vision of God's vast, all-pervading love for us, making us and keeping us human, underlies all the writings in this collection, whether about art and music, or Cicely Saunders and the hospice movement, or the combined holiness and *folie de grandeur* of Mervyn Stockwood, or the exasperations of being Church of England, or our responses to AIDS and illness.

It is the vision that made Michael Mayne the man he was: kind, open, warm, accepting, humane, compassionate and deep. It would be too much to claim that it is an exclusively Anglican vision; but it has characterized Anglicanism at its best. We badly need it still, for the Church's sake and for the world's.

Introduction

There are times when we need to share our stories as a way of
affirming our common humanity and helping to authenticate
what others may be going through.
Michael Mayne

Michael Mayne (d. 2006) wrote five bestselling books, each
marked by his passion to communicate in an increasingly
impersonalized and secularized culture the importance of
remaining open to the Mystery of the Word made flesh, the
Christian message: God was in Christ. A priest of the Church
of England, Mayne wrote for readers of deep faith or none:
for practising Christians, but equally for those haunted by
the idea but struggling to experience the reality of God's
love. Though located in the heart of the established Church,
Michael Mayne was ever reaching out to those on its margins.

Mayne was clear that his vocation was primarily that of
pastor, not writer. He went so far as to say that, for him,
'pastor' was the most beautiful word in the English language.
While his books had been warmly received, and had never
gone out of print, at his death he left behind thousands
of pages of unpublished sermons, addresses and lectures.

A Skilfully Woven Knot: Anglican Identity and Spirituality is
a collection of ten writings, five of which are published here
for the first time. The five previously published pieces will
be unfamiliar to the majority of Mayne readers. The works
date from 1985 through to 2004 and reflect the breadth and

depth of Mayne's spirituality. His was a pastoral heart and, in words he once used to describe one of his mentors, Mervyn Stockwood, Mayne himself was 'a priest to his fingertips'.

In an address honouring Dame Cicely Saunders, Mayne observed: 'Pioneers in any field are protesters against the status quo.' From within the Church of England, and while loyal to her, Michael Mayne exercised a prophetic ministry in an era of great social, political and ecclesiastical change. He was prophetic on issues of inclusion and was a pioneer in the Church's evolving response to the AIDS crisis. He grasped that the Church's apprehension of truth is 'a growing thing', that 'the tradition we inherit is a living reality' and not just a game of 'pass the parcel'. Mayne's spirituality was heavily Christocentric. In his own words: 'God discloses himself in a life ...' For Mayne, the hallmark of Jesus' own spirituality was that he gave each person he met his full attention. Mayne's own pastoral ministry was thus oriented towards recognizing that each individual is of unique and unsurpassed value in God's eyes and is therefore 'literally irreplaceable'. As a parish priest, religious broadcasting executive, as Dean of Westminster, and in an active retirement, Mayne pushed the Church he loved to evolve and adapt in a changing landscape so that the gospel could, in one of his favourite phrases (from Martin Luther), 'console and enliven' in a culture increasingly indifferent to, or even hostile towards, the institutional Church. Michael Mayne's pastoral voice retains its capacity to console and enliven.

Part 1

Addresses

1

A Skilfully Woven Knot

Ordained Local Ministry Training, 3 August 2004

For ten years I found myself responsible for the liturgy and
the spiritual life of a building, which is at once both the most
Anglican of churches and the most ecumenical: Westminster
Abbey. That is to say: it is regarded throughout the world as
the spiritual heart of the Church of England, the place where
kings and queens have been consecrated and crowned for 1,000
years, and where most of them lie buried; and the church in
which great services are held that touch on the life of the nation
and therefore need to be ecumenical and even sometimes
multifaith, and indeed may be broadcast worldwide – such as a
royal wedding, or the funeral services for Princess Diana or the
Queen Mother. Yet my primary concern was that the ordering of
the liturgy at the Sunday and weekday Eucharists, the preaching
of the word, the choice of music, and the saying and singing
of the Daily Offices, represented Anglican worship at its best.

It was also the most ecumenical of churches in that day by
day thousands of tourists from all over the world and from
many different traditions came to the Abbey, many of them to
join in the worship. For the main Eucharist every Sunday there
would be some 500 people present from many different nations
and traditions: French, Italian and Spanish Roman Catholics,
Old Catholics from Scandinavia, Dutch Reformed from South
Africa, Orthodox from Moscow, Mennonites from Iowa, and
Baptists (thousands of them) from Texas. As I stood at the door

I was often asked – especially by Roman Catholics – 'We are puzzled. What are you – Protestant or Catholic?' And I would reply, 'In a sense, we are both. We are *catholic*, in that we believe in the continuity of the Church of England as part of the worldwide church of God, and place a high emphasis on the sacraments, with the Eucharist as central to our lives; we wear vestments, and sometimes we use incense. But equally we are *protestant* in that we protested against the abuses of the Church at the time of the Reformation and do not recognize papal authority or his infallibility in matters of faith and morals; and we give a high place to the importance of Scripture and the ministry of the word. In a word, we're Anglican.' And, though I said it much less pompously and more accessibly, they would frown and shake their heads and go away even more puzzled than before.

A regular demand on the Abbey is to devise memorial services for those who have contributed in a major way to our national life: everyone from a Prime Minister to a great artist, actor or footballer. It might be Harold Macmillan one week, and Laurence Olivier or Bobby Moore the next. And, like those endless parish funerals in church or at the crem., the departed may or may not have had any obvious Christian belief. And it seemed to me wonderfully Anglican that we had the freedom to devise a different style of memorial service for each: one that met the demands of integrity, both for what we believed and also for the unique person being remembered. And that was the strength, not the weakness, of the Church of England.

The other week in *The Observer*, Will Hutton, not normally sympathetic to the Church, wrote of a memorial service held in St Bride's, Fleet Street, for their former news editor, attended by many in journalism and politics:

who wanted to spend an hour to honour a man we respected and loved. But notably in a church. Few of us in a secular age manage a deep-felt commitment to religious faith, but once again the Church of England had opened its doors to a group of scarcely religious people with whom it had the slightest of relationships but who needed the combination of shrine and liturgy to express a deep appreciation of somebody they had loved and lost ... Twice this year I have found myself in different Anglican churches: once at the funeral of a friend who had died of breast cancer, the other at the funeral of my father. And once again, the same Anglican culture seeped from the walls. The openness is but one component of a relaxed, profoundly tolerant faith that kindly accepts our fallibilities and which is fundamentally reassuring at moments of loss. Our collective relationship with the Church of England runs very deep. I concede my attachment to the church is as much cultural, attracted by its inclusiveness, kindness and tolerance, as any faith I may have. It represents, for all its weaknesses, the best of England. It is about being open to everyone in all their imperfect and sometimes non-existent relationship with faith.

'Inclusiveness, kindness and tolerance': in defining the Anglican spirit no one could have put it better. And I'll come back to those deeply attractive qualities. For first, we must dip our toes into the past. Not that I want to bore you with facts that you have studied and know as well as I do; but maybe a brief refresher will do no harm, especially as, if we want to go forward into any future undivided Church, then the steps that have got us where we are have to be understood and incorporated into where we are going next. Unless, of course, we subscribe to John Betjeman's reactionary cry: 'Thy Kingdom come, from see to see, Till all the world is C of E.'

So how did it emerge, this Church of England, which has spawned a worldwide communion of 70 million Anglicans in

164 countries, of which the Archbishop of Canterbury is *primus inter pares*, first among equals? The *1066 and All That* answer is that it came about because King Henry VIII wanted a male heir and needed a papal decree of nullity for his marriage to Catherine of Aragon in order to marry Anne Boleyn. Impatient at the long delay, Henry married Anne, was at once excommunicated, and in his turn rejected papal authority and in the Act of Supremacy in 1534 declared himself 'the only supreme head on earth of the Church of England, called *Anglicana Ecclesia*'. But history is never so simple, and Henry's desire to take on the papacy and curb its power was simply the occasion that dates the recognition that the religious life of Europe was in the midst of the most profound and traumatic upheaval.

On the Continent, the Reformation challenged a Church that was mired in abuse and corruption, and was the product of a new theological dynamic, a new discovery of the gospel in all its primitive freshness and power. In Germany, Martin Luther was protesting against the corruption of Rome and the great abuses attending the sale of indulgences. He called for a radical reform of the religious orders, and an equally radical shift of emphasis from the preaching of salvation in terms of good works to one of the sheer grace of the love and forgiveness of God as seen in Jesus Christ. In Zurich, Ulrich Zwingli was calling for similar papal reforms, and after his death the more extreme and puritanical John Calvin in Geneva became the founder of a movement that was to sweep across Europe and become synonymous with a church tradition that sees the Scriptures as the sole rule of faith, which believes in great simplicity of worship, and absolute predestination.

But corruption was not confined to the Continent. In England there was graft, simony and indiscipline. Henry VIII's physician, Linacre, had been rector of four parishes, canon of three cathedrals simultaneously and precentor of York, and all before he was ordained priest. Cardinal Wolsey, Henry's Chancellor, kept a mistress by whom he had a son who was made, while still a schoolboy, Dean of Wells. In France, the Archbishop of Sens only entered his cathedral for the first time when he did so in his coffin. That great Renaissance prince, Pope Julius II, put himself at the head of the papal armies in Italy, and the Archbishop of York commanded one of his regiments. The great scholar Erasmus (whose translation of the Greek New Testament was to have a profound effect, sending people back to the source of their faith) also wrote a scurrilous pamphlet of Pope Julius arriving in heaven and being met by St Peter, where the following conversation takes place:

> The Pope: Open the door quick. If you had done your duty you would have met me with the full ceremony of heaven.
> St Peter: You seem to like giving orders. Tell me who you are.
> Pope Julius: You recognize me, of course.
> St Peter: No, I've never seen you before, and at the moment I find the sight quite extraordinary.

The fact that Julius was the patron of Michelangelo does not seem to have worked in his favour.

By the middle of the sixteenth century the English Church was ripe for reform. It had been planted by the Romans in the third century, expanding under the Irish and Scottish Celtic influence of St Columba and St Aidan, and in the south under the Roman influence of St Augustine, in the sixth century. It had its rich monasteries, its cathedrals and its parish churches in every town and village. Now, in the turmoil of reform, Cambridge was to be the centre of scholarly renewal, where not only Erasmus was Lady Margaret Professor of Divinity, but the heads and fellows of colleges included Matthew Parker at Corpus, Nicholas Ridley, Hugh Latimer and John Whitgift at Trinity Hall, and Thomas Cranmer at Jesus. With the invention of printing, folk could own their own Bible for the first time and read it in the vernacular in their own homes; and Owen Chadwick writes how it became possible for 'the brazier, the feltmaker and the coachman – the working people – [to go] into the Bible to fetch their divinity for themselves'.

While Henry VIII suppressed the wealthy monasteries and ordered the English Bible to be set up in churches, he only tolerated the new spirit of Protestantism up to a point. It was not until after his death, when the young Edward VI became King, that doctrinal Protestantism became the official ecclesiastical policy. Within a year or two, Archbishop Cranmer issued his incomparable Book of Common Prayer, devising (from the seven monastic Offices) the two Orders for Morning and Evening Prayer. It is still the classic statement of the ethos of the Church of England. He also drew up the Forty-Two Articles of religion, which were to form the basis of the later Thirty-Nine Articles, which defined the policy of the new Church of England in relation to the controversies that were still raging. Edward's short reign was followed by that of the Roman Catholic Queen Mary, who restored the papal supremacy; and it was only the accession of Elizabeth I that finally established the Church of England. Elizabeth sought a comprehensive settlement that would embrace all her subjects. She had a characteristically English aversion to extremes, and sought a middle way, a reconciliation between papists and Puritans, between those who looked to Luther and Calvin and those who looked to Rome. But they were turbulent years, a time of religious ferment, in which a number of remarkable men finally guaranteed the emergence of an established Anglican Church and set its defining marks. Let me name five of them.

First: John Jewel, Bishop of Salisbury in 1560. He had fled to the Continent under Mary's persecution, for he strongly opposed the Church of Rome, taking his stand on the teaching of the Church Fathers of the first six centuries.

In his great work *Apologia Ecclesiae Anglicanae*, he affirmed that by the sixth century the clear outline of Christian doctrine had been drawn, and that all further development must be found within that outline. He is the first to set out the Anglican claim that in faith and order the Anglican Church is continuous in identity with the primitive church.

If Jewel led the defence against Rome, the defence against the Puritans was in the hands of an even greater man, Richard Hooker. The scholarly Hooker first gave the Church of England a solid intellectual basis. His great book *Of the Laws of Ecclesiastical Polity*, has a tolerance and largeness of view that was quite new in religious debate. His book is a defence of the Christian faith and also a discussion of the Order of the Church and the relationship between Church and state. He argued for the identity of the one with the other, in one Christian nation ruled by one monarch and under one law. His great contribution is his defence of reason; reason for Hooker being that faculty within us that makes it possible for us to receive the revelation of God whenever and however he speaks. And Anglicans ever since have placed great importance, in matters of faith and morals, on those two human faculties: reason and conscience.

Hooker's ideas were carried to their logical conclusion by the third and fourth of my great defining Anglicans: William Laud and Lancelot Andrewes. Laud, a learned, choleric and really rather unlovable man, the son of a Reading cloth-merchant, became Archbishop of Canterbury in 1633, moving to Lambeth with his Smyrna cat and his tortoise. He is the key figure in developing the ethos of the Church of England. He was Catholic in sympathy and his fine mind was matched by great skill, plus a certain ruthlessness, as an administrator. He was a great tidier-upper. His great contribution was a belief in ordered freedom: his ideal being the dual principle of a *decent uniformity* in worship, and a *wide liberty* of theological speculation. He insisted that churches be kept in good repair, with the altar restored to the east end, and ordered all bishops to hold visitations in their dioceses, and, set up his own agents to make sure they conformed. Laud believed passionately that liturgical uniformity was the precondition of theological liberty, and he sought to enforce the observance of the Book of Common Prayer by setting up the court of High Commission. The latter was widely regarded as an Anglican form of the Inquisition; and when Charles I fell, Laud found himself in the Tower, and was beheaded four years later, aged 72, before a jeering crowd, and after a moving affirmation of his belief in the Church of England, and a plea for forgiveness for all his faults.

If Hooker had defended the use of reason against a slavish bondage to narrow interpretations of Scripture, and if Laud imposed order on the Church, my fourth defining Anglican, the gentle, wise, unambitious Lancelot Andrewes, claimed for it a proper place in the Church universal, and infused it by his practice of prayer and his teaching on the Eucharist, with a deep and strongly Anglican spirituality. I feel very close to him, for he was Dean of Westminster and lived in the same medieval house as I did, and he was court preacher to both Elizabeth and James I. He chaired the committee that met in that Deanery to translate the King James version of the Bible. The book of his own personal prayers (his *Preces Privatae*), published after his death, has been perhaps more widely used by Anglicans than any book of prayers outside the Book of Common Prayer. What Cranmer was to our public liturgy, Andrewes is to the world of private devotion. Andrewes went on to become Bishop of Chichester, Ely and Winchester, and his contemporary, John Aubrey the diarist, tells of how at Winchester he would find out who were his faithful clergy trapped in poor livings. One such was Nicholas Fuller, Minister of Allington in Wiltshire, and Aubrey writes: 'The Bishop sent for him and the poor man was afraid and knew not what hurt he had done. [The bishop] makes him sit down to dinner and, after the dessert, there was brought in, in a dish, his institution and induction and the gift of a prebend – which was his way.' Lancelot Andrewes was a man of huge learning and ecumenical spirit, and William Laud called him 'a great light of the Christian world'.

Seven years later there died in the tiny village of Bemerton my fifth and last of some of those who helped define the ethos of the Church of England. As a boy at Westminster School, George Herbert was much influenced by Dean Lancelot Andrewes. Herbert was a Fellow of Trinity College, Cambridge and Public Orator at the University when Archbishop William Laud persuaded him to become a priest, and for the last three years of his life he served as Vicar of Bemerton. There were two small churches, both in disrepair, and he was often ill, yet not only did he compose some of the finest religious poetry ever written, in which he lays bare his doubts and fears as well as his conviction of the overwhelming love of God and the power of his grace, but he also wrote, in *The Country Parson*, the classic description of what it should mean to be a faithful pastor in the Church of England. Izaak Walton, who wrote about the lives of John Donne, Richard Hooker and George Herbert, said of *The Country Parson*: 'It is so full of plain, prudent and useful rules that every country parson that can spare twelve pence and yet lacks it is scarce excusable, because it will both direct him what he ought to do, and convict him for not having done it.' In his classic book *Anglicanism*, Bishop Stephen Neill writes: 'One who wishes to know what *Anglicanism* is and has not much time for study cannot do better than to study the life, the poems and the prose of George Herbert.' John Aubrey writes of his contemporary Herbert, in his inimitable way: 'He married Jane, the third daughter of Charles Danvers Esquire, but had no issue by her. He was a very fine complexion and consumptive. Marriage, I suppose, hastened his death.'

Since then the two strains of Church belief and practice that fought for predominance at the Reformation, the pattern of Geneva versus the pattern of Rome (the emphasis on the word versus the emphasis on the sacraments; the desire for simplicity versus the richness of ritual and ceremonial; the emphasis on good works versus the emphasis on grace) have been ever-present. Like those little model houses you buy in Switzerland that indicate the weather, where either a tiny man or a tiny woman emerge to show if the sun is going to shine or if it is going to rain, so the evangelical and the catholic traditions have fluctuated within our Church, with John Wesley and Charles Simeon and the Evangelical Revival, with Keble and Newman and the Oxford Movement; and in the main the national Church, both Catholic and Reformed, has managed to contain them.

What, then, are its defining marks? As part of the one, holy, catholic Church we believe that there are *four* such marks: the Bible, the creeds, the two gospel sacraments of baptism and the Eucharist, and the threefold ministry. We believe that the Scriptures contain all that is necessary to salvation. But if those are the marks of episcopal churches worldwide, what is the unique and characteristic ethos of the Church of England, the skilfully woven knot created by the Elizabethan Settlement?

1. We are a Church that seeks to balance word and sacrament in our central acts of worship. The Eucharist lies at the heart of that worship, balanced by Morning and Evening Prayer. That is the influence of Thomas Cranmer.

2. *There is a particular form of quiet but profound Anglican spirituality*, centred on the Scriptures and the Eucharist. That is the influence of Lancelot Andrewes and George Herbert.

3. We place great importance on *human reason and individual conscience*. There is a strong tradition of scholarship, of thought and enquiry, combined with a belief that each person ultimately must, after thought and guidance, make his or her choices and be responsible for their own actions. That is the influence of Richard Hooker.

4. A belief in the *via media*, the middle way. The Preface to the 1662 Book of Common Prayer is a classic statement of the Anglican ethos, and not just in terms of liturgy: 'It hath been the wisdom of the Church of England ever since the first compiling of her Publick Liturgy, to keep the mean between the two extremes, of too much stiffness in refusing, and of too much easiness in admitting any variation from it.'

We believe in moderation and toleration in our continuing search for truth. But this is not mere compromise, a bland sitting-on-the-fence, though at its shallowest it has often been just that; but rather it has to do with the nature of our history and recognition that the search for truth is more complex than we always allow. We believe that the truth is larger than any one of us, that no one person or party or church holds a monopoly of it. We believe that the truth rarely lies in this extreme view or that extreme view, nor does it lie somewhere in the middle, but it may live, paradoxically, in both extremes. This is our refusal to be partisan, to say 'I am right: you are wrong'. Any form of intransigent fundamentalism or biblical literalism is alien to the true Anglican spirit of toleration. And so the Church of England, seeking to be true to the skilfully woven knot of the Elizabethan Settlement, has always been slow to condemn extreme views, preferring to hold together people of the most diverse opinions. And Anglicanism is not to be judged by its extremists.

5. Which brings me to the fifth and final mark of Anglicanism, and that is its *comprehensiveness*. To some, such an extreme variety of views within one Church suggests weakness: others know it to be a strength. We are very different people, with different experiences and needs and personalities, and this affects how we perceive God and how we choose to worship him. There are truths that, though essential to the fullness of the gospel, may not be easily combined, and in loyalty to Christ we endeavour to hold together those who cannot at present agree. Within our history all movements and traditions – catholic, evangelical, liberal – have brought their own particular truth to enrich the whole, and at different times one or other tradition has been dominant. At present it is the evangelicals who are in the ascendant, but I believe that the best and wisest of Anglicans knows that he or she must endeavour to be evangelical *and* catholic *and* liberal in the best sense of those words. For this in the end is what the Church of England stands for: the catholic understanding of the continuity of the Church and the central place of the sacraments in the body of Christ; the evangelical understanding of the importance of the word of God, of conversion and of the central place of the cross; and a truly liberal freedom of thought and conscience, with a desire to be open to other people's understanding of truth. These are the things that Anglicanism, where it is most true to itself, has been able to hold together in a creative and dynamic tension. That is its own particular genius, and perhaps its most important contribution to the one, holy, catholic Church.

But it doesn't always make for an easy life. In a paper presented to the bishops of the Lambeth Conference in 1988, the Scottish theologian Elizabeth Templeton spoke of the tensions raised by matters of grave disagreement and the Anglican way of coping with them:

> I have been constantly struck by the best generosity of your recurrent insistence that across parties, camps, styles and dogmas, you have need of one another. Both internally and in relation to other evolving Christian life forms, you have been consistently unclassifiable, a kind of ecclesiastical duck-billed platypus, robustly mammal *and* vigorously egg-laying. That, I am sure, is to be celebrated and not deplored.

In his first Presidential Address as Archbishop of Canterbury to the General Synod, Rowan Williams said:

> Being an Anglican Christian now is to offer a hospitable place for a wide variety of people engaged in spiritual exploration. We have never been bound by confessional statements in the way other churches have; we have a special relationship with the cultural life of our country, and we coax people towards a spiritual life that draws on the most sensitive and creative dimensions of what is natural to them, and try to encapsulate that in appropriate liturgies.

The theologian Paul Avis has written:

> The vocation of Anglicanism is to create the climate of spiritual liberty in which individuals may witness to the truth as they see it, submitting themselves to the criticism of their peers without fear of ecclesiastical criticism or censorship, the only condition being their continued voluntary participation in the worshipping life of the Church and outward profession of (their) baptismal faith.

If I were now to tease out the application of the Anglican ethos in terms of the new situation we face in the disputed areas of the ordination of women priests and bishops, and the implications for the whole communion of the consecration of Bishop Gene Robinson, I should not just be overrunning my allotted time but trespassing in eternity. So let me just say this: I am glad to belong to a Church that is open to the work of the Holy Spirit. St John writes of Jesus in his last discourse on the night before he died saying that the Spirit will lead us into all truth, and that 'the spirit blows where it wills'. I understand those words as meaning that a theology grounded on the unchanging scriptural truths of God revealed in Jesus as Christlike, and a Church seeking to be faithful to the words of Jesus and seeking the life of the Kingdom with its unchanging values of justice, forgiveness and compassion, must nevertheless accept that the Spirit works through our developing understanding of the creation and its creatures, not least genetics and gender. Even Richard Hooker saw the Church as an organic, developing body, within an organic, changing society. The Spirit works to enable a changed understanding of certain truths to come equally from the grassroots as from the top, and enables new developments. The Church of England has managed to contain within it people of profoundly differing views, finding its strength not in a bland uniformity but in something much more precious: unity in diversity. The unity forged by the reality that at the deepest level we are even now one in Christ.

John Betjeman's 'Thy Kingdom come, from see to see, Till all the world is C of E' is more than a bit over the top, but we see what the old boy meant.

2

The Transfigured Commonplace

United Church, Winchester, 2004

Can God be perceived through the arts? There's no ambiguity about what I'm being asked to address. Leaving the choice of subject to the speaker can be risky. Some years ago a distinguished academic was invited by the Cambridge Christian Union to speak on 'whatever lies closest to your heart'. They assembled, Bibles at the ready, eyes shining, notebooks open. 'What has lain closest to my heart throughout my long life', he began, 'is the Romney, Hythe and Dymchurch Railway.' In a recent American exhibition 100 artists were asked to illustrate how they saw God. It included a public urinal, a corpse and a videoed face on a pillow repeatedly saying: 'Don't kill anybody!' It was suggested that their deeply secular response was partly the impossibility of the challenge, and partly their fear of being associated with religious fundamentalists. As well they might be. To ask whether we can perceive our elusive God through the arts at once invites three questions: What sort of God is God? What sort of creature am I? And what sort of creation lies all about us? And in attempting some answers I am only too aware that a fish can have no concept of the vast expanse of the ocean, nor can a bookworm nibbling on a single page of *The Brothers Karamazov* have much concept of Dostoevsky. When I use the term 'the arts' or 'the artist' I mean all those who use their creative talents to illuminate our lives, and while time doesn't permit me to include dance or theatre or film or opera or photography or popular music, I reject the concept of 'high art' and 'low art', preferring John Tusa's distinction of 'reflective' art and 'entertainment' art. Inevitably, this address is about the former – though I've written it with a background of Haydn, Cole Porter and Billie Holiday.

So what kind of God is God? While I believe God to be the source of my life and the ground of my being, who (in St Paul's words) 'has not left us without some clues to his nature', I know I must in fact live with paradox: the paradox of One who is both the unimaginable, unknowable Other, and also the intimate, immanent and incarnate God, in whose image I am made and whose creation and whose creatures carry haunting echoes of his presence. Like art, theology is the attempt to express the inexpressible; as T. S. Eliot said of poetry, it's a 'raid on the inarticulate'. But herein lies the challenge. I can remember Michael Ramsey 30 years ago warning a group of middle-aged clergy that we were living at a time where people had less and less understanding of the transcendent, of that which is (or of One who is) other and greater than we are, whose Being presses human language to its limits – and beyond. Yet to deny the transcendent flies in the face of the whole human story. For those who have sought seriously to contemplate the mystery of our existence and speak of encounters that touch on the very source of their humanity quickly realize that the world perceived by our five senses is only a partial aspect of reality. That underlying all we are and know is (for want of better words) a Diving Ground. Paul Tillich speaks of God as 'the infinite and inexhaustible depth and ground of all being'; Martin Buber says that 'God may only be addressed not expressed'; Dietrich Bonhoeffer, writing from his prison cell, describes God as 'the Beyond in our midst'. Which means, in short, living with paradox. It means remaining properly humble in the face of the mystery and ultimately the unknowability of God, the *via negativa*, while also pursuing the *affirmative way* of discerning a God who not only creates us in his image but invites from us a response, a relationship. In short, we need to name him.

The Bible tells of a God who speaks out of a profound silence: 'In the beginning was the Word'; of how in time the Old Testament prophets haltingly define the qualities they believe God possesses: his oneness, his Law, his justice, his mercy. On that the three great Abrahamic faiths of Judaism, Islam and Christianity agree. But Christianity then makes a further leap of faith, claiming that, in a moment of time, God says: 'I give you my Word: I give you myself.' The Word, the Logos, the deepest, innermost expression of God's being, is 'made flesh and dwells among us, full of grace and truth'. This Word, says John, has God in it as your words, if they come from your heart, have you in them, have in them your breath and your feel and tell of who you are. And in describing Jesus as 'the one who lies closest to the Father's heart' he is saying that if God was ever to communicate the truth of his inmost nature, the only truth we need to know, he could only do so in our language, and on our terms. Human terms. In the shape of one who came to be called Emanuel, 'God with us'. In the shape of a life and death whose meaning is self-giving love; and who claimed that self-giving love is of the very essence of one who is best addressed as Father. It isn't that in Jesus we have an exhaustive picture of the transcendent Being we call God, but authentic glimpses of the one whose Love undergirds the creation. We can't look directly at the sun, but by its light the world is illuminated, and at times transfigured. So God transcendent and God immanent, his mystery and his availability, must be held together if we would know the truth. Further, as St Augustine discovered, there is only one place in the universe where God waits for us to find him, and that is at our own centre; and having found him there, we can go on to find signs of his presence everywhere, incarnate in his world.

So what kind of creature am I? An ensouled body; an embodied spirit. I am a single, integrated and unique entity seen from three particular angles. I am *body*, within which 50 trillion different cells are working away to keep me alive, my unique twisting double helix of genes connecting me with my parents and grandparents and my children's children. And I am *mind*, I am me thinking, using my 3lb brain with its 15 billion nerve cells and 100 million neural links, in which are miraculously stored the ability to laugh and to cry and fall in love, and dream dreams and feel compassion, and to imagine and observe and create works of art. For I am also informed and animated by *spirit*, which gives me a recognizable and consistent integrity until the day I die, and that makes my whole much greater than the sum of my parts. The poetry of Genesis tells us that we are the end-product of a God who in Eden takes the dust of the ground and breathes into it the breath of life. Scientists put it differently. They tell us that in the unimaginably long process of evolution, what was once stardust became a sea cucumber and then a whale and then a baboon and, finally, not just any old creative human being, but Wolfgang Amadeus Mozart. Stardust became Shakespeare; and Michelangelo; and Johann Sebastian Bach. The most mysterious of our human qualities is that of the creative imagination; so that to ask 'What is art? What is music? What is poetry?' is to ask 'What is a human being?' And to reply: 'When Rembrandt works his magic by recreating with profound compassion a lifetime's journey in a human face; when Cezanne enables you to see a mountain or an apple with new eyes; when Shakespeare or Yeats or Seamus Heaney so spin their web of words that they strike the heart at a magic angle, in what has been called "the word become gooseflesh"; and when Bach in his *Goldberg Variations* or Schubert in his C Major Quintet produce sounds that stand somewhere between matter and spirit and cause in us a kind of wondering stillness, why, then, we are faced with what Hamlet calls "the heart of our mystery"'. We are faced with aspects of ourselves that seem both authentic, timeless and universal – what W. H. Auden called 'breaking bread with the dead'; and it changes our view of the world. To speak of the greatness of Homer or Plato or Shakespeare or Tolstoy or Milton or Rilke, is to speak of writers who saw into the heart of what it means to be human. For we all share the same human story. Shakespeare said things about love and pain and grief and jealousy and forgiveness that are as fresh and meaningful and true as the day he wrote them. When Ibsen was asked where he found his plots he said he found them in the Bible and the newspapers, for the problems, predicaments and delights of mankind are unchanging. 'My paintings', said Marc Chagall, 'represent the dreams of all humanity.'

So what sort of creation is it in which we are set? Modern cosmology tells a story of supreme beauty and order in the laws of nature: a complex yet elegant harmony so delicately balanced that it enabled life to emerge. The ordered structure of the leaf, the crystal, the atom. Now the Hebrew mind knows no distinction between the material world and some separate 'spiritual' one; the Spirit blows where it wills and as God names his creation, he sees that it is good and takes delight in it. 'The whole earth is full of his glory,' says the psalmist. In Gerard Manley Hopkins's words, 'The world is charg'd with the grandeur of God. It will flame out like shining from shook foil.' It is a creation in which everything is capable of acting as a sacrament of God's presence, one in which, if we know how to give it our attention, the holy is revealed in the ordinary. And it is this sanctification of the ordinary that pervades the teaching of Jesus, and is reflected by the poet Douglas Dunn in his lovely phrase on keeping a 'rendezvous ... with the transfigured commonplace'. William Blake saw 'a World in a grain of sand,/ And a heaven in a wild flower', and believed that 'Everything that lives is holy'. 'I think of the world as Blake did,' writes the novelist Jeanette Winterson, 'as a glorious thing, and through art – painting, music, poetry – we connect with the real world, with the luminous, the transcendent.' This is not pantheism, identifying God with nature, for that would be to deny his transcendent otherness. It's what is called panentheism, the belief that every part of the universe is pervaded by God and moment-by-moment sustained by his Being. In the words of Martin Buber: 'To look away from the world, or to stare at it, does not help (us) to reach God; but he who sees the world in Him stands in his presence.' In her desire to show that God is not just the creator, but the lover, of all that exists, Julian of Norwich famously took a tiny hazelnut to demonstrate the presence of God in this one delicate aspect of creation and to recognize that in the end all that is flows out of the love of God and that all is mystery. So experiences of God are experiences of the ordinary seen in the context of the otherness that enfolds and lies within them; the discovery that the ordinary is the miracle, and that everything, from black holes to the birth of a baby, *is both simple and profound depending on how much attention you give to it.*

So we come to the core question: given this sort of God and given a creation that bears witness to its Creator – Can God be perceived through the arts? I'm assuming that we accept that religion and spirituality are not one and the same. Those of us who choose to be religious seek, through words and music and silence and sacrament, to relate to our Creator. And for centuries sacred choral music, from the haunting beauty of Gregorian chant, a motet by Byrd or Tallis, a Passion by Bach or the mystical tones of John Tavener, has been a powerful medium for bridging the human and the divine. And the religious art of Giotto, Titian, Raphael and Bellini; from Rubens's *Crucifixion* and Piero's *Resurrection* to those of Craigie Aitchison and Stanley Spencer, by focusing on the implications of the Word made flesh, have centred the prayers and enhanced the devotion of generations of worshippers. But others feel no need to express their spirituality in formal religious belief and practice. 'Music', writes George Steiner, 'has long been the theology of those who lack or reject any formal creed.' And as regular churchgoing has declined, a great deal of what one might call 'implicit spirituality' has been left to flourish in its wake.

'Spirituality' has come to mean everything from the mystic's dark night of the soul to the products of Glastonbury's largest New Age bookshop, the Psychic Piglet. The playwright Dennis Potter once bluntly said that 'Anyone who claims to be totally uninterested in any sort of spiritual response to the ache of life is little more than a narrow-headed thug.' And some neuroscientists now speak of us possessing potentially three different kinds of intelligence: not just what are known as IQ and EQ – our *intelligence* quotient and our *emotional* quotient, that lifelong dance of head and heart – but also SQ, our *spiritual* quotient. A high spiritual lifelong quotient doesn't imply religious faith. What it does mean is that we are more likely to have a sense of the beyond, the transcendent, and to respond to the arts. It's interesting that in the context of the modern hospice, with its emphasis on the treatment of spiritual, as well as physical, pain at the end of life, many now speak of 'secular spirituality', by which they mean that all human beings as they grow older are haunted by the question: 'Has my life a purpose and a meaning?' And the best hospices are using the arts more and more to help people discover and express aspects of themselves – their inner spiritual journey, their deep centre – even in their final days.

For the purpose of this address, I'm using 'spirituality' to mean anything that nurtures the human spirit. And nothing nurtures the human spirit more profoundly than the arts. They are gratuitous, pure bonus. We don't need them to keep us alive, yet we need them if we are to be fully alive. As the poet A. E. Housman said a century ago: 'the yearning for the beautiful and the good is no less native to (us) than the craving for food and drink, and (when this craving is starved) part of (us) dies (and we) walk lame to the end of (our) life'. Art is in the blood and in the brain and the genes. In every culture, from the most primitive to the most sophisticated, people have told stories, sculpted from wood and stone, and decorated surfaces with colour. And for me, the secret that causes the scales to fall from our blinded eyes lies in the word 'wonder'. By 'wonder' I mean that uniquely human sense of awe: awe that anything at all exists rather than nothing; that no two snowflakes are alike, that even a blade of grass is full of mystery. It is to feel in the rush of the passing the stillness of the eternal. And wonder begins and ends with the simple yet demanding act of *giving attention*. Once it came naturally. As infants, seeing each new person or object for the first time, we gave each our absorbed and delighted attention, but that gift soon deserted us; and it is the artists – the poets, painters, composers, sculptors, dancers, actors, novelists – who have taken time to wonder at and delight in what lies before their eyes – in Wordsworth's words, 'to see into the life of things', and who have best expressed what it feels like to be human.

'Beauty and grace are performed', writes Annie Dillard, 'whether or not we notice them. The least we can do is to try to be there.' There's a whole universe out there waiting to be noticed, admired and loved and wondered at, and artists urge us to pay attention to it, and learn to love it in what the spiritual writer Pere de Caussade called 'the sacrament of the present moment'. Our spirits may be fed in many ways: by silence; by words and images; by the shape of certain buildings or light playing on stone; by the natural world; by music. An artist's take on the world may put us in touch with unsuspected depths within ourselves. And it is this endeavour to give attention that links the arts and spirituality: a spirituality that recognizes God's presence in what lies before our eyes. Think of the Celtic Church, and the Ignatian and the Franciscan traditions, and their emphasis on the sacredness of creation and our contemplation of it as a place where we encounter the divine. If prayer is about giving attention to God in stillness, alone or in the company of others, then art galleries and museums are spaces where we give attention to images that it has seemed important to each age to capture in paint and stone and clay. Concert halls are spaces where together we give attention to what has been thought important to capture in music that is created anew with each performance. Theatres are spaces in which together we concentrate as the playwright illuminates the agony and the ecstasy, the humour and the pathos, of the human journey. And artists have learned to use their inward eyes and ears to open themselves not just to the meaning of the human condition, but to those small epiphanies that can illuminate our journey, what Virginia Woolf called 'moments of being ... little daily miracles, illuminations, matches struck unexpectedly in the dark'. 'Art,' writes the novelist Joseph Conrad:

(is the) single-minded attempt to render the highest kind of justice to the visible universe, by bringing to light the truth underlying its every aspect ... to find in its forms, in its colours, in its light, in its shadows ... what ... is enduring and essential – the very truth of their existence. My task ... is to make you hear, to make you feel – it is, above all, to make you see. That – and no more; and it is everything.

So, before the artist marks the canvas, moulds the clay, or juggles with the a and the b and the c of the alphabet, he or she must spend time becoming immersed in the world: with an observing and a listening that is like bird-watching; for how can they report accurately on the mystery of the tiger, the kestrel, or a human face, without this kind of wondering attention that is akin to love? It is when something as ordinary as a sleeping child, as common as a cowslip, suddenly commands our attention, so that we are face-to-face with the truth of it (not simply the truth *about* it) that an experience of the numinous and the transcendent may occur. This is to glimpse what Hopkins called the '*inscape*'; by which he meant that each flower, each tree, each animal, each person, has its own unique *proper inward measure*, its intrinsic value, its true God-given self. And each exists in its own way; is *good* in its own way; is *beautiful* in its own way. So Hopkins looked at cloud formations, or the shapes of icicles, or a bluebell, and saw in each both their unique 'thisness', and their 'otherness', which was for him a sign of the Creator's artistry. The poet Rilke writes to a friend:

> I love in-seeing. Can you imagine how glorious it is to in-see a dog, for example … to let yourself into the point from which it begins to be a dog, the place in it where God, as it were, would have sat down for a moment when the dog was finished, in order to watch it … and to nod that it was good, that nothing was lacking, that it couldn't have been better made.

'Reflective' art seeks to capture – in a poem, a painting, a sonata, a sculpture – the passing transient moment with a contemplative awareness of an underlying mystery that has to do with the underlying reality. So George Herbert writes: 'A man that looks on glass/ On it may stay his eye;/ Or, if he pleaseth, thro' it pass,/ And so the heaven espy'. Rilke said that his aim was to lift objects out of time and make them what he called 'capable of eternity': what the art critic Andrew Graham-Dixon calls its ability to give us a sense of 'the instant elsewhere'. Though, in the immortal words of Picasso: 'The great artistic problem is how to get something of the absolute into the frog-pond.'

So we read the poets and novelists in the hope of finding

words that confirm what we know intuitively (but haven't found the words for) about the way a bird flies, or a tree grows, or how a loved face looks; or about what it feels like to be in love or to be forgiven or consumed by grief; and some of us read George Herbert or Thomas Traherne to learn about the nature of grace or what it means to say that God is Christlike. And we look at painters who see the spiritual in the everyday: Rubens praising the sheer exuberance and beauty of the natural world; Turner seeking to capture the wonder of light; Michelangelo rejoicing in the beauty of the human form bursting from the stone, what T. S. Eliot calls 'the soul of man that is joined to the soul of stone'. Van Gogh, who said he couldn't look at a painting by Rembrandt without believing in God, writes to his brother Theo: 'I want to paint men and women with that something of the eternal which the halo used to symbolize, which I seek to convey by the actual radiance and vibration of my colouring.' Stanley Spencer, with his deeply spiritual vision of the divine and the mundane as coextensive, sees Cookham as a heaven on earth, with Christ being baptized in Odney Bathing Pool, and early morning swimmers looking on with mild surprise and a proper English reticence. When the artist Winifred Nicholson painted a vase of lilies-of-the-valley she said they held 'the secret of the universe', much as Jesus of Nazareth said that the wild anemones exceeded Solomon in all his glory.

And what of music? For many, it's the most spiritual of the arts: something is being said through music, with its rhythm, melody and harmonies, that only music can say. Certainly it has the power to invade, and touch, and even heal the human heart. The world draws boundaries: music sings of the ineffable and indefinable, and it is no less real. I mean, how can a note on a manuscript in Debussy's *La Mer* convey the whole feel of a calm sea at dawn or in a raging storm? (Of *La Mer*'s three movements, the first is subtitled 'From dawn to noon'. The composer Eric

Satie told Debussy that the best bit occurred 'at a quarter to eleven'.) Nor can the effect of music just be described as a succession of feelings, for it also conveys a kind of knowledge. When Mozart advised his friend Haydn not to come to England because he couldn't speak the language, Haydn replied: 'But all the world understands my language.' We can't explain just how a succession of sounds, with its melodies and harmonies, work on the brain to silence us, or move us to tears, or give us delight, or comfort us in adversity, and will perhaps console us when we come to die, but we know music relates to something essential about our humanity. And certain music not only speaks with a universal tongue, for musicians (like writers and artists) do that most Godlike thing: *they bring order out of chaos*. And it is order, form, that gives everything we know about its own identity, its own proper shape, its glorious particularity. We delight in each person, each thing, being its familiar (if mysterious) self, whether it's someone we love or an oak tree or a Bach sonata. For centuries people have believed that the created order of society reflects an underlying divine order in creation (what was once thought of as the music of the spheres). So that when composers pluck out of the sea of sound melodies and harmonies that seem to us beautiful, significant and true, they not only create order out of chaos but help persuade us that ours is an ordered and trustworthy universe undergirded by certain unchanging laws. So Kingsley Amis could write of Mozart: 'Other composers can make me feel their joy, sorrow, fury, high spirits; Mozart affects me rather differently. What he offers is … a series of glimpses of a state of perfect order.' And, I would add, an extraordinary kind of rightness and inevitability.

Which brings me to my home stretch. Press me as to what has motivated my life and I would settle for one word: the word *authentic*. The search for that which I can trust because it rings true in the deepest part of my being. It *feels* right. It wins from

28

us an unconditional 'yes!' It's this 'rightness', this inevitability, this intrinsic authority, that is the most striking factor in the greatest art. The canons and fugues of Bach proceed step by step to an inescapable conclusion, and we can't imagine that they could be different. *'Muss es sein? Es muss sein'* ('Must it be thus? It must be thus') is the inscription Beethoven placed at the beginning of one of his late quartets; and we may feel of them, or, indeed, of *King Lear* or Durham Cathedral or a Rembrandt self-portrait: 'Yes; it has to be like that.' And where the arts convey this sense of rightness it helps us say 'yes' to life as it is: sometimes painful, often bloody, always unpredictable; but also joyful and full of beauty. And I believe such an affirmation only makes sense if life is grounded in a transcendent, objective reality that is *absolute in meaning and value*, and of which the creation and certain works of art give us glimpses. If we are made in the image of God who is the ultimate source of beauty, goodness and truth, then it is as if in the depths of our souls we carry an icon of that Beauty, that Goodness, that Truth, and that wherever we glimpse these things we find an echo of that ultimate reality. For, whatever a currently fashionable postmodernism would have us believe (and fashions pass), there are certain objective truths in the world – like prime numbers in mathematics – that, once discovered, are true for ever; certain abstract truths that exist independently of the minds that grasp them. And down the ages an unchanging intuitive moral sense of right and wrong, like concepts of love, truth and beauty, is part of what it is to be human. We make the same kind of moral judgements as the Greeks did. Plato taught that beauty, with its implicit harmony, balance and wholeness (as in the concept of the 'Golden Mean') is the way God manifests himself to our senses and, indeed, that you can be changed by the object of your contemplation. Archbishop William Temple said that 'to be conscious of absolute value and the absolute obligation that

29

it imposes is to be aware of something ultimate in the universe', and my claim is that the best artists, writers and musicians not only explore matters of ultimate human concern, but help us come a bit closer to the Creator's heart expressed in his creation. Which is why we should listen to them. In Peter Shaffer's play *Amadeus*, Salieri says of Mozart's music: 'This was a music … filled with such longing that it seemed to me that I was hearing the voice of God.' I like to think that God has placed us on earth not to judge us, but to enjoy us, to enjoy not least our creativity, and that our obligations to him are no less aesthetic than moral. And I have no doubt that the arts are part of God's self-revelation, and that when they succeed in awakening in us some sense of transcendent beauty or joy or peace or harmony, this is because they are grounded in the Truth, grounded in God.

So, a final word. We live in a world that seems to be governed by fury, where the wells of peace are poisoned and the cries of the suffering are largely ignored. Seamus Heaney speaks of how the arts can help redress the balance, serving as a constant reminder of 'a glimpsed alternative' – like the Christian faith is a reminder that there is a world elsewhere. That the horrors of war and the dehumanizing acts of the wicked don't annihilate beauty, destroy art, overthrow truth or abolish love. Bernard Levin had for years been suffering from a severe form of Alzheimer's. In almost the last essay he wrote, on Christmas Eve 1994, these are the words with which he ended – and with which I, too, will end:

> The eternal verities are not changed, not even damaged, by the wickedness and despair. Providing that we do not try to deny the terrible reality, there is no shame in retreating to the Schubert quintet, to Shakespeare's Sonnets, to the *Rondanini Pieta* of Michelangelo. Whatever Christmas means to us, from nothing to everything, it will last for ever. And love, the best republic, may weep, but will abide.

I would claim that Levin's 'beloved republic' is a monarchy: it is the beloved Kingdom, where Christ reigns, with its great abiding and eternal verities – love, justice, mercy and truth; and *they will abide*.

3

A Very Healthy Kind of Truth

Baylor University Forum,
20 September 1993

I have been here before. Two years ago I stood in this impressive theatre having had a very close encounter the day before with a rattlesnake. My wife and I had been invited out to a farm a few miles away so that we might relax before facing the rigours of Baylor Forum …

Westminster Abbey is an amazing place. When the state of Texas was created 150 years ago the Abbey was celebrating its 800th anniversary. The present building dates from the thirteenth century and is just coming to the end of a massive 20-year cleaning and restoration programme so that it looks as gleaming new as the day on which it was built.

Forty-one Kings and Queens have been crowned in the Abbey, everyone from William the Conqueror in 1066 to Queen Elizabeth II in 1953; and twenty-nine of them are buried there, some in magnificent royal tombs. There are famous writers like Chaucer and Tennyson and Charles Dickens and Robert Browning buried in Poets' Corner, and each year members of Baylor representing your Browning Library come to lay a wreath on Browning's tomb. We have the tombs of scientists such as Isaac Newton and Charles Darwin – about 4,000 people in all, some of them famous, some quite unknown, are buried within our walls.

When people come to the Abbey there are two things that seem to grab their attention most of all. The first is the Coronation

Chair where all the monarchs have been crowned; but the second is something quite different. It's the grave of a nameless, anonymous man. It lies in the most public place, in the floor of the nave just inside the great west door through which everyone enters; and the extraordinary thing is that every time a head of state comes to London, he or she comes to the Abbey on the first day and lays a wreath at the grave of that unknown man.

Let me tell you his story, for it's a very moving one and contains a very important truth. All I can tell you about him, this man who has no name, is that he joined the army to fight in what was probably the bloodiest and most wasteful of the wars of our time – the First World War, the Great War of 1914–18. It was a war largely fought out in the trenches, in the mud and blood and barbed wire of France and Belgium, where the trenches were placed so close to one another that the troops on either side could hear each other talking. It was a war in which no cost in human lives seemed too great for the very smallest of advances.

On 1 July 1916, at 7.20 in the morning, a large mine detonated beneath a ridge in Northern France. For the next ten minutes the British troops in their trenches, almost all of them volunteers in their first experience of war, followed their orders: they did nothing. This gave the Germans time to come up from their shelters underground and man the machine-gun position in a line facing the British trenches. When at 7.30 a.m., according to plan, the British climbed out of their trenches to attack and walked into no-man's-land – they had to walk, running was forbidden – with their rifles at the slope, the Germans mowed them down. The British went on with their assault; the Germans went on killing them; until the trenches got clogged with the bodies of the men, many of whom had never even made it over the parapet. The slaughter continued all day, and it went on, unbelievably, for the next seven days. At the end of the first day alone the British army had lost 60,000 men: by the end of the week, the losses were such that it worked out at one man killed for every single foot of a 16-mile line. It was the beginning of the Battle of the Somme which lasted three months, and at the end of those three months British losses alone were more than half a million men.

You might have thought that casualties on that scale would have caused those in command to stop and question what they were doing. It seemed to have the reverse effect. More and more men were thrown into the fighting, and the end of the war found the British and the German nations decimated, with many of the most gifted of their nations slaughtered like cattle. One day in 1920 the then Dean of Westminster wrote to the British King, George V, saying that he had a letter from an army chaplain suggesting that the finest possible memorial to those who had died would be for the body of an unidentified soldier to be dug up from among the hundreds of thousands whose bodies lay in shallow graves under the soil of France and brought back to England to be buried in the Abbey. The King, who was not blessed with much imagination, turned the idea down. The Dean persisted and managed to get the support of the Prime Minister, Lloyd George. The King grudgingly agreed and on the early afternoon of 9 November six small working parties, each carrying tools and a plain coffin, set out for the six main battlefields. Nameless corpses were chosen from the forest of rough crosses all marked 'unknown', and the bodies were then sealed in the coffins and driven back separately in six ambulances. They were placed in an army hut, and that night an officer who had never previously been inside that hut was blindfolded and led to the door. He went in and groped around until his hand touched a coffin. That was how they chose the poor nameless man whose body within a few weeks was to be followed through the streets of London in a procession led by the King walking on foot, and along streets lined with thousands of silent people. He was then buried in the Abbey at a service

34

described by the London *Times* as 'the most beautiful, the most touching and the most impressive this island has ever seen'.

As I say, the grave lies just inside the main door. The coffin is made of English oak, it's buried in French soil, and the black marble slab is Belgian with letters on it taken from melted down bullet casing of the First World War. It's surrounded by a border of poppies that grew thickly on the graves in France.

We don't know his name. We don't know his rank. We don't know his age. He could be anybody's son or husband or father. Yet he has come to represent all those who lost their lives, not just in that First World War but in the other wars of our time. Here is an unknown man who has become much more famous than all the famous people who surround him.

Now that seems to me a very healthy kind of truth. For it says two things and it says them very powerfully:

1. It makes a statement about the appalling cost of war in terms of human lives. It doesn't say that war is never justified. It doesn't say that their self-sacrifice was in vain. What it says is that, though war may sometimes be inevitable, it is always evil because it diminishes human lives and cheapens them, so that men and women become simply means to an end rather than ends in themselves.

2. But the second thing we are saying in honouring that unknown man also has to do with the value of people. It says that you have no right to distinguish between the ordinary and the extraordinary, because each person is extraordinary, and only the blindest, most unobservant person could fail to see the wonder of a human being; that the millions in every country who have been mown down in the wars of our time are unique and irreplaceable individuals, each of them made in the likeness of God.

In order to make that truth even clearer, when the Gulf War started we threw a spotlight on the Grave of the Unknown Warrior and we moved in front of it a large crucifix, so that as people came in the door they saw the grave and they saw the man hanging on a cross. And that was our way of saying: Christians don't believe in a God who is distant and remote and uninterested in his creatures. We believe in a God who chose to reveal the secret of his inmost nature in the only way we could possibly grasp it: in human terms, in the words and actions of the man called Jesus. And what Jesus reveals is one who loves us as a father loves his children and values us for the unique individuals we are more than we can ever imagine.

For isn't that what drew people to Jesus: the value he put on every individual he met? They watch him as he heals and forgives and consoles and encourages and loves all he meets, and takes that love to the very limit by refusing to be silenced and dying in agony on a cross. And those who knew him best came to understand that in him they were seeing God's self-portrait, and that the only accurate description of God is that he is Christlike.

Two years ago I stood here and tried to speak about the God in whom I believe, the Christlike God whose spirit is within us, and who shares in the joys and sufferings of his creation. Afterwards *The Lariat* gave me the rather surprising headline: 'Abbey Reverend Summarizes God's Character'. I doubt if even the Pope would dare to do that. But when I came out of the Forum and walked back through the campus I suddenly saw chalked on the sidewalk – along with messages advertising meetings and tennis tournaments – these words: 'Jesus wept. Is your God man enough to cry?' Whoever wrote those words had put in one sentence all I had struggled to say, and they are dead right.

But the point I am making is not so much about the nature of God as about the nature of human beings. About your worth, your value; about the fact that there's never been anyone like you nor ever will be again: you are literally irreplaceable. And that's why we have to treat one another with care. And that's why it pleases me that it would seem the two things that people remember most when they leave the Abbey are the Coronation Chair where each new King or Queen is crowned and the grave where we honour the dead body of the man who doesn't even have a name.

The great Indian leader Mahatma Gandhi once said: 'If you don't see God in the very next person you meet there is no point in looking for him further.' And Jesus made it clear that in the end only two things matter: that you love God with all your heart and that you love your neighbour as yourself. He also spoke about those who live in the light and those who live in the darkness – those who had learned to see and those who were still blind. So let me end with an old Jewish story

One day a Rabbi asked his students: 'How can we determine the hour of dawn? How can we tell when the night ends and the day begins?'

One of his students suggested: 'When from a distance you can distinguish between a dog and a sheep?'

'No,' answered the Rabbi.

'Well,' said another. 'Is it the moment when you can distinguish between a fig tree and a grapevine?'

'No,' said the Rabbi.

'We give up,' said the students. 'What's the answer?'

'The moment when the night ends and the day begins,' said their teacher, 'is when you can look into the face of other human beings and have enough light in you to recognize them as your brothers and sisters. Until you can do that, for you it's night, and you are still in the darkness.'

4

A More Compassionate and Humane Society

A Tribute to Cicely Saunders

I take as my text some typically blunt words from the late playwright Dennis Potter: 'Anyone who claims to be totally uninterested in any sort of spiritual response to the ache of life is little more than a narrow-headed thug.'

Over a good many years I've visited the United States. Whether in Texas or New York, Washington DC or South Carolina, I have invariably been asked three questions: 1. Do you know the Queen? 2. Do you know the novelist, Susan Howatch? 3. Do you know Cicely Saunders? And often asked them, I might add, in the reverse order. To the first the answer has been: 'Yes, for Westminster Abbey is the Queen's church and she was my boss'; to the second, 'Yes, for the Abbey is the church in which Susan Howatch worships'; and as for Dame Cicely, 'Why, yes, a thousand times yes; and for many years I've been proud and privileged to be her friend.'

I first visited Cicely in 1967 in the brand-new St Christopher's, as a parish priest increasingly concerned with the dying and the bereaved, to quiz her on her concept of palliative care. Fifteen years later, I invited her to the University Church in Cambridge one Sunday night where she had an illuminating dialogue with Brian Redhead. Five years later I was at Westminster Abbey, when Cicely invited me to serve on St Christopher's Council and where I had the delight of working on the services held in the Abbey for the Hospice's 21st anniversary and for its Silver Jubilee. And, like countless others, I have learned from Cicely to look at death and our understanding of the needs of the dying with new eyes.

Now, I want to attempt two things: first, to seek to summarize those aspects of Dame Cicely's philosophy that have been instrumental in making St Christopher's Hospice the epicentre of the international hospice movement, and then to speculate a little on the continuing relevance of what seems to me the motivating force of her teaching. As all may now see from her letters, her seven years at St Joseph's, during which she was introducing and monitoring pain and symptom control and raising the money to build the first research and teaching hospice, enabled her to do that primary thing: to listen to the dying. It deepened her belief in their spiritual needs: for security, for meaning and for a sense of self-worth. Her vision of effective palliative care coupled tough clinical science with empathy and compassion. In her own words, it demanded: 'a commitment to openness to and from the world; a commitment to the mind, to research, learning and intellectual rigour; and the recognition of the vulnerability of one person before another'. Pioneers in any field are protesters against the status quo: in Cicely's case it was a protest against the pain, neglect and isolation that were (and still can be) the lot of the dying.

Now if people's needs and their potential are to be met as fully as possible, then there must be a recognition that those needs are physical, emotional, social and spiritual. And it is the spiritual needs of the dying that Dr Saunders affirmed from the start to be as relevant to atheists as to believers: the need we all have to find a meaning in life. Faced with those existential questions we need to search, to question, and to be (in her words) 'listened to with respect and answered with honesty'. Much influenced by Victor Frankl's seminal work *Man's Search for Meaning*, Cicely wrote of spiritual pain, or soul pain, which can take the form of a deep anger at the unfairness of what is happening to you and what has led up to it, together with what may be a desolating sense of meaninglessness. When we are sick, and especially (I guess) when we are dying, we need to bring some kind of order and design to what feels like chaos and a falling-apart of our whole familiar world. At such moments we may need someone beside us who will listen to our stories and help us interpret and make sense of them. So Dr Saunders was convinced that there must be not only efficient pain control, but a concern for the immediate family, and a readiness to be there, to offer help as the patient reflects on their inner griefs or guilt or longing, to stop and listen to whatever pain is being expressed and to stay with it. For in this unity that is 'me', my emotional pain can, of course, have a powerful effect on my physical pain. 'Hospice' was to recapture the ancient sense of the words 'hospital' and 'hospice': to be places where you experience hospitality, to have (unlike many large and anonymous hospitals) a sense of home. At its best it was to become a place of healing. I believe people were drawn to Jesus of Nazareth because he gave them a sense of worth; he gave them his full attention and assured them that they were loved by God for their own unique selves. And in that affirmation lay the beginning of their healing. Whether or not God is part of our personal equation, all of us need affirming, in large ways and small. How wonderfully affirmed I felt, incidentally, on my last visit to hospital for an X-ray as I stood nearly naked in a tiny cubicle where the art therapist had caused to have inscribed and framed on the wall Shakespeare's words, 'Shall I compare thee to a summer's day?' I was brought back to earth by the notice beneath it that said: 'Have a word with one of the nurses if you think you may be pregnant.'

People need affirming, especially when they are dying, and all of us in the caring professions are in the affirming business; and we have to use whatever tools lie to hand (words, a hug, a hand held, a listening ear, a shared silence, music, art, poetry) to explore memories and seek to heal them, and so relieve people's pain. If in our dying we are trapped at the surface level of our minds we are cut off from the healing power of our own inner depths: that deep centre, at once intimate and strange, that is the essence of who we are. This deep psyche is at once a dustbin for unwanted thoughts, emotions, old hurts and painful memories, but also the potential source of our healing: a place of powerful inner resources and childlike spontaneity. And because the vocabulary of the unconscious is image, symbol and myth, stories, painting and music can put us in touch with unsuspected aspects of ourselves, and speak to us at the deepest level of harmony, beauty and order.

I think of two patients who died within this past year in a small hospice. Mary, a 40-year-old mother, was dying of an aggressive cancer. She was angry, depressed and deeply manipulative. She was visited by the young poet-in-residence who suggested she should try to write a poem expressing some of her anger and pain. She didn't respond. Ten days later, when she died, they found in her locker a handful of moving poems with a note asking for these to be given to her husband as they said things she had never before been able to express. Then there was Jim, a completely circular bricklayer, his body covered with tattoos. Jim had an advanced cancer. Inarticulate, he was encouraged to paint a picture for the first time in his life. To his own (and his family's) amazement, he produced a series of delicate watercolours, revealing a side of himself he had never been encouraged to explore. In each case, as you may imagine, those two people left in their wake quite a complex grieving process for the hospice's bereavement counsellors.

When Cicely spoke in my church with Brian Redhead 20 years ago she used the phrase for her approach to each dying person that I shall always identify with her: 'You matter because you are you, and you matter to the last moment of your life.' Her particular vision grew from her own deep Christian faith. In those early days, as St Christopher's slowly evolved, questions of its religious orientation and the nature of the community she wished to establish needed to be talked through and written about. And 'community' was always a pivotal concept, with an increasing emphasis over the years on the diverse membership that an effective community, committed to a common cause, can contain. The original *Aim and Basis*, as drawn up by Dr Olive Wyon in 1965, did not mince words:

> St Christopher's is founded on the full Christian faith in God, through Christ. Its aim is to express the love of God to all who come in every possible way ... with respect for the dignity of each person as a human being, precious to God and man. There are no barriers of race, colour, class or creed ... It is planned that the staff should form a community, united by a strong sense of vocation with a great diversity of outlook in a spirit of freedom ...

It affirmed that 'love is the way through, given in care, skill, thoughtfulness, prayer and silence'. That Statement was discussed every few years, and it was still, with minor alterations, in force in 1988. Even ten years ago the brief included these very explicit words: 'St Christopher's was established and has grown as a Christian foundation, not simply in terms of its care but from a belief that the God revealed in Christ shared and shares the darkness of suffering and dying and has transformed the reality of death.'

In a changed cultural climate, such language is no longer the most sensitive or appropriate way of defining the hospice brief. Yet few would deny that Dame Cicely's perception of the nature of spiritual pain is spot-on, nor that the hospice ministry is to human beings with spiritual, as well as physical, needs. Indeed, some hospices now speak of a 'secular spirituality', by which I take it they mean that spirituality is not necessarily to be identified with religion. Many who work in them would not see a recognition of the spiritual as implying a belief in God or a need to respond to a creative Spirit whom members of the major world faiths believe to be the source of their life and the ground of their being. For what does it mean to be human? It means to be an embodied spirit. Some scientists define human beings in terms of stunningly complex electrochemical machines; yet being human doesn't *feel* like that. If we're lucky in life's lottery, it feels more like what the psalmist hints at when he says that we are 'fearfully and wonderfully made': that we fall in love and dream dreams and let our imagination roam and create works of art; that we value good, seek justice, feel compassion, experience delight; that we have a sense of the transcendent, a kind of hunger of the spirit for beauty and for truth. But being human also means knowing sickness of body and mind, and relationships that turn sour, and the hurt and anguish of loss and deprivation.

Being human means I am an indivisible unity: body, mind and spirit. But those three words don't describe *separate* bits of me, but rather *a single integrity seen from three particular angles*. I am body: a physical organism, ageing fast, tall and increasingly bald, occupying my own bit of space. I am *mind*: I am me thinking, me using my 3lb brain to write these words, a brain which contains some 15 billion nerve cells (more than the population of the globe). And I am also *spirit*. When you sit beside a dying person and observe the moment when the last breath is exhaled, you realize with awe the immediate qualitative difference between a corpse and a body informed and animated by spirit. There is about me a uniting, life-giving spirit that makes me much more than the sum of my bodily parts. No net of words can capture me: for there is always some mystery remaining.

So being human means we are on a double journey: an *outer* journey and an *inner* journey, which match our outer and inner worlds, our landscape and our inscape. The *outer* journey has to do with visible landmarks: with the place of our birth and childhood, the houses where we have lived, our work, our family, our illnesses, our cars, our computers and our dogs. When we come to die these are the memories we shall recall, for they help define us. But the *inner* journey, which in the end is the one that matters most, has to do with more subtle things: with our *feelings*, with love given and received, with words like forgiveness, compassion, fulfilment, creativity; with what we believe and what we hope for. To speak of *spirituality* is to speak of this inner journey, of the existential questions, of the meaning of it all, and of those values and concepts that we believe to be of ultimate value. And the challenge we each face, in our living and (especially) in our dying, is how to integrate the two: how to bring together our outer and our inner landscapes into the integrity that is me.

This is why St Christopher's was founded; that is what a good hospice stands for, and will always stand for: a desire to affirm each individual as they come to die with a sense of their own unique worth. And when the great achievements of the twentieth century come to be properly assessed, I believe that Dame Cicely's vision and pioneering work will come to be seen as one of the greatest of them, a significant step in the creating of a more compassionate and humane society.

Part 2

Sermons

5

On a Huge Hill

1991

In February 1985 Great St Mary's, Cambridge (where I was vicar), and the Roman Catholic Chaplaincy were the centre for an ecumenical Teaching Week called Encounters. We aimed at a presentation of Christian belief that was thought-provoking and honest, an interpretation of life that took account of its mystery and its daunting mixture of good and evil. Not least we wanted students to understand better the legitimate breadth and space of faith and discipleship and the need for diverse and complementary insights in our encounters with God.

The main speaker was Archbishop Robert Runcie. He was not chosen because he was Primate: he was chosen for his ability to engage both mind and heart and communicate with wit and conviction the faith that sustains him; for his sense of the mystery of things; for his own infectious humanity.

This is a sermon I preached in Great St Mary's on the prior Sunday, and I dare to hope that it is true to the spirit of that type of Anglicanism that the Archbishop best represents.
Michael Mayne, 1991

The Times once published a thoughtful first leader on the subject of doctrine and belief in the Church of England. 'In recent times', it said, 'no slur against the Church has been more damaging than the charge that an Anglican may believe anything or everything

– or nothing. And nothing would be more bracing to the Church than to regain the sense that there are truths worth living by and even dying for, and that the Church of England rests on a solid bedrock of sure faith.'

Looking to the future, Jesus said to his disciples that 'the Spirit of truth will guide you into all truth', and 'you will know the truth and the truth shall set you free'.

In one of the sermons he preached in Trinity College Chapel, Harry Williams makes the distinction between two kinds of truth: what he calls the 'outside' kind and the 'inside' kind. The first kind is what universities are concerned to teach. They train people to observe objects and encounter ideas with accuracy and imagination and see how they relate to one another, and the mastery of a subject by one who has become expert in at least some aspect of it may be publicly recognized by conferring the degree Master of Arts or Master of Science.

But there is another sort of truth that is less easily defined and that can't be mastered in this way. The 'inside' sort. Truth that can't be kept at a distance and that has little to do with the marshalling of factual information. This kind of truth comes from outside us and claims us, and at its core there is a heart of mystery. It may be described as a kind of visitation to which we are invited to respond.

Think of something of great beauty: a painting or a poem or a concerto. You can master the outside of it, analyse its content and structure, the way the notes of music or the words lie on the page or the paint on the canvas, but having done all that there remains a quality, a beauty, a truth that claims you and that may even judge you; and you can only respond to this mystery with a kind of wonder.

Now the truth of God is like that: the 'inside' sort of truth. For the mysterious truth of God is that he is self-giving Love, and the response to love, like the response to beauty, is a matter for the heart, for an inner response of our whole being. 'I do not know the truth', wrote Kierkegaard, 'except when it becomes part of me.'

But where do we find the truth of God that we are to make part of ourselves and that we are judged by? In the Church? If so, in what tradition of the Church, speaking as it does with such diverse and confusing voices? In the Bible? If so, in what parts of the Bible, for it gives us no consistent answers? And so the deeper question we must ask is: 'What is this truth that has created both the Bible and the Church?' And the answer is quite clear. Truth is not what we think or say about God. Truth is what God has done and is doing.

The truth is Jesus Christ. God discloses himself in a life that, writes St John, 'is full of grace and truth'. 'I am the truth,' says Jesus. 'He', writes St Paul, 'is the image of the invisible God.' So the truth of God centres on this life, this death and resurrection; and it is learned in the common life of the community that sprang from those events. And the Christian life is a pilgrimage where, as we learn to be open to the Spirit at work within and among us, this truth is slowly apprehended and made part of us.

Today we recognize that the creeds, those attempts in the early centuries to capture what Christians most deeply believe about God, are expressed in fallible, shifting, limited human language drawn from the Bible and the early Christian councils. They contain different kinds of statements – some historical, some symbolic or poetic. For the New Testament writers and the Church Fathers were well aware of the paradox Christians always have to face: the more we come to understand God, the more we become aware of the ultimate mystery of his Being.

For the present, all our insights into the truth are partial ones. Yet sadly, such is the nature of our insecurity, each one of us behaves as if *my* insight, *my* experience, *my* understanding is more valid than yours. In social or political terms truth becomes the way *I* see it; and unhappily, when it comes to religion, truth tends to mean 'my Catholic understanding of the nature of the male priesthood' or 'my conservative evangelical understanding of salvation', with scores of little minor fortresses in between. So, for example, we have the recent passionate demand that all bishops should be asked to subscribe to the truth of the Virgin Birth; or we have some hardline members of the Christian Union in Cambridge circularizing all other members and urging them not to take part in next week's Teaching Week as Roman Catholics are involved and 'the true gospel will not be preached'.

Now I take my stand on what that *Times* leader calls 'the solid bedrock of sure faith': the belief that God was in Christ, reconciling us to himself, that his nature is love, that I am created in his likeness, that my sins are forgiven, that God (in a new creative act) raised Jesus from the dead and invites me to work for his Kingdom. But I also believe that the truth of God is infinitely greater than all our individual perceptions of it and that we only begin to apprehend what it is by looking at what are the insights of *this* tradition and what are the insights of *that* tradition and saying, 'Yes, you are right; and yes, *you* are right, too!' I am Anglican because it gives me room to breathe in the tolerant air of a Church that, in its pursuit of truth, allows its members a wide liberty of theological speculation, and because it believes that no one person or party or church has a monopoly on the truth; and that this comprehensiveness is not the weakness of the Church of England, but its strength.

How could one feel anything else standing in this pulpit? I cannot think there is a parish church in England that was so closely involved in the events of the Reformation, and the hammering out of the Church of England ethos under the Elizabethan Settlement, and in the succeeding centuries. This university played a critical role in the development of the English Church, and all its most influential theologians preached within these walls. Cranmer, Latimer, Ridley, Whitgift,

Matthew Parker, Lancelot Andrewes – all were Masters or Fellows of Cambridge colleges. What we call Anglicanism is a deeply scriptural faith, with equal emphasis on the word and the sacraments. Its form was greatly influenced by the intellectual collision between the Bible-loving Puritans and the High Church Sacramentalists in Cambridge in the sixteenth and seventeenth centuries. Later, Charles Simeon, vicar of our neighbouring parish of Holy Trinity for nearly 50 years, was one of the leaders of the evangelical revival; and Westcott, Lightfoot and Hort, all Cambridge men, between them worked to establish those principles of biblical scholarship that have had such a profound and liberating effect on the whole Church of God.

Those groups of Christians who look for a kind of authoritarian, absolute, bullet-proof, cast-iron certainty about everything are therefore not typical of the spirit of the Church of England, with its long history of freedom of scholarship and its appeal to reason. No other Church allows its members so much spiritual freedom, and at its best shows the strength of toleration and comprehensiveness.

By toleration I mean a willingness to suffer for the time being what may appear to be error. And a refusal to be partisan (which is so much easier), preferring to allow wide interpretation of doctrine. 'Comprehensiveness', said the report of the 1968 Lambeth Conference, 'is an attitude of mind we have learned from the controversies of our history. It demands agreement on fundamentals, while tolerating disagreement in matters on which Christians may differ without feeling the necessity of breaking communion ... It implies that the apprehension of truth is a growing thing ... and there must be a continuing search for the whole truth in which the Protestant and Catholic elements will find complete reconciliation.' As Charles Simeon wisely said: 'The truth does not lie between two extremes, but in both extremes.' And throughout its history various parties and traditions have made their contribution to our Church: evangelical, catholic, liberal. They still do, and we are the richer for it.

Let me give you just one example of what it means for there to be what has been called, by William Temple, 'the utmost liberty of thought that is compatible with the maintenance of spiritual fellowship'. In the Doctrine Commission Report published 50 years ago, a committee under the chairmanship of Archbishop William Temple published a note on different views of the Virgin Birth in the Church of England. They said that, for many, the Virgin Birth speaks of an act of sheer graciousness on the part of God, the fact that in Jesus humanity makes a new beginning: here is God breaking into history and inaugurating a new age. 'Many of us hold the belief that the Word made flesh is integrally bound up with belief in the Virgin Birth, that this will increasingly be recognized.'

But others, believing that a child inherits his or her genes and chromosomes jointly from both father and mother, and believing that Jesus was a true human being like us, think that our Lord's birth took place under the normal conditions of human generation. 'In their minds,' said the Report, 'the notion of a Virgin Birth tends to mar the completeness of the belief that in the Incarnation God revealed Himself at every point in and through human nature.' And they go on (and these are important words for us to remember in our present angry disputes): 'We recognize that both these views ... are held by members of the Church ... who fully accept the reality of our Lord's Incarnation, which is the central truth of the Christian faith.'

I chose to call this sermon 'On a Huge Hill'. The words come from a poem of John Donne:

On a huge hill,
Craggy and steep, Truth stands, and he who will
Seek him about must, and about must go.

Many people want a kind of certainty, and you can buy it in various fundamentalist or other authoritarian stores. But that kind of certainty does not seem to me what the New Testament means by 'faith' or 'truth'. It is not that kind of openness to new apprehensions of truth of which St Paul speaks when he says, 'Now I see through a glass darkly, now I know in part, but (one day) I shall know even as I am known.'

There is a nice story of Bishop Westcott, who so valued speculation as an approach to truth, being met in Cambridge by one of his pupils, who said to him: 'Thank you. Thank you, Dr Westcott! You have made everything perfectly clear to me.' 'Oh!' replied Westcott. 'I hope not! I hope not!'

What we have tried to do, in setting up this Teaching Week in Great St Mary's, is to enable those who are searching for God at all kinds of levels to hear men and women of different traditions – Roman Catholic, Anglican, Methodist, Baptist – speak of how God in Christ has encountered them. The speakers will not attempt to thrust down others' throats their own understanding of truth: all they can hope for is that others will discern in them an authentic experience of God and then, in their different ways, seek to make it their own.

6

Conviction and Openness

Sermon Preached at the Requiem Eucharist for
Bishop Mervyn Stockwood at All Saints,
Clifton, 27 January 1995

In 1958 Mervyn preached a course of sermons on 'The Faith Today' in Great St Mary's, Cambridge, which ended with these words: 'In a village church is this epitaph on the tomb of a cavalier soldier: "He served King Charles with a constant, a dangerous and an expensive loyalty". '

It is entirely fitting that Mervyn's funeral should take place here, for not only was it his wish, but it was in the pre-war All Saints that his spiritual journey began. 'I always think of All Saints with deep affection', he wrote. 'As a child I felt at home there, and in it I began to develop a sense of mystery ... Later it taught me the dignity, beauty and reality of corporate worship.' In fact, its catholic teaching and liturgy implanted beliefs about the sacramental nature of the world and the centrality of the Eucharist that were to inform his whole ministry. Nothing in his school or undergraduate years, certainly not Westcott House where he was blissfully happy, was to prepare him for the trauma of the East End of Bristol in the late 1930s and during the war. It was the experience of St Matthew Moorfields, with the acute unemployment and distress, the homelessness and squalor he found there, that made him a socialist and a city councillor, that sharpened his concept of the Kingdom and that deepened his strongly incarnational belief that nothing divides the sacred and the secular, and that the fact of God's sovereignty is to permeate the whole of life.

And St Matthew Moorfields did one thing more: it drew out of him a profound pastoral compassion that, 25 years later, was to cause the clergy of Southwark, though they might criticize him at times for his showmanship, and grumble at times at his idiosyncrasies, to love him dearly for his pastoral heart. I guess I am one of the very many who believe that Mervyn has helped them to become better priests.

Mervyn often said that his happiest days were those at Great St Mary's, Cambridge. They were four years that encapsulated his strengths in a setting that was tailor-made for him: a dispirited run-down church, a liberal, intelligent and questioning congregation, dons to be diverted by his originality, and undergraduates to be challenged by his views and captivated by his words. He knew our highest truths to be but half-truths, explorations into mystery, and he preached with an invigorating mixture of conviction and openness. He established the parish communion as the central weekly event; and he initiated the informal Sunday night services with a range of unpredictable speakers that were to continue until five years ago. Twenty years later I followed him at Great St Mary's, and whenever people spoke of Mervyn they smiled, because they had such fond memories.

I was Mervyn's first, and longest-serving chaplain; and I suppose none came to know him better than his successive living-in chaplains. We saw the challenge, and the cost. And in particular the cost to him, in many ways a lonely and vulnerable figure, with all the normal human strengths and weaknesses; yet somehow, by reason of the force of his personality and his complex, contradictory nature, both his virtues and his faults were a little larger than life. And very different messages were received by the world and by those who witnessed his more hidden ministry; and both were true.

He did enjoy the trappings of office, and mixing in the

corridors of power, and he could appear at times impossibly pompous and overbearing; but he usually listened when his chaplains told him so and in private he was the kindest, the most thoughtful and companionable of men; and, as I can vouch, when it came to visiting and encouraging the sick, ministering to the dying, or counselling those in trouble he was a priest to his fingertips. But the paradox remained. Driving everyone else to their knees by talking into the small hours, he was invariably on his knees in his chapel a few hours later. A lover of good food and wine, he was the most hospitable of men, rating hospitality to be a hallmark of Christian witness. He entertained generously, imaginatively and on a broad scale, not least his clergy and their wives, and the civic leaders of the enormously varied Southwark boroughs; and when he left Bishop's House there were 9,000 signatures in his visitors' book.

And did he have style! Who else but Mervyn would have successive dinner parties for three party leaders, Harold Macmillan, Hugh Gaitskell and Jo Grimond to meet the newly appointed Archbishop Michael Ramsey? Who else but Mervyn, hearing the Scottish Moderator had presented Pope John XXIII with a stone from the Dead Sea, would have taken to the Vatican the largest Easter egg he could find, gift-wrapped and on a silver charger, and told the papal chaplain it was the head of John the Baptist? Who else but Mervyn would have preached his first sermon at Great St Mary's on Isaiah's words: 'If you must bore men, well and good; but must you bore your God also?' Who else but Mervyn would have spent the whole night in prayer in Southwark Cathedral before his enthronement; or arranged for a bottle of iced champagne to be delivered to Lambeth each time the Archbishop returned from a daunting overseas tour; or left a decanter in his will to an evangelical friend 'provided he undertakes to use it for alcoholic drinks'?

To be Mervyn's chaplain was hard work. It was physically and sometimes emotionally demanding, but it was an education into the workings of the Church of England (and how he loathed its bureaucracy!); and occasionally it was a revelation of what it meant to go the second mile. But, above all, it was fun.

I remember one day Mervyn returning from a funeral of a Southwark priest who had died young. Archdeacon Sam Hayman had given the address. 'It was so good,' said Mervyn. 'He simply set John's life and ministry in the context of the timeless sacrifice of the Mass, and that said it all.' For Mervyn, the daily Eucharist encapsulated his whole ministry. It was about his readiness to share Christ's life of self-giving love, supremely revealed on the cross. It was about bringing ourselves and our world under God's sovereignty as the bread and the wine are taken, identifying ourselves with the broken, self-offered body of Christ as the bread is broken, and sharing in a foretaste of the Kingdom of God as we become the holy community, kneeling side by side at the altar rail. 'This is the tempo by which we live,' he wrote; 'daily offering ourselves to God, daily allowing Christ to confront us and knit his personality with ours; daily identifying ourselves with his sacrifice as we pursue the way of self-giving love; daily doing what we can to make the world in which we live the holy community … and the risen Christ meets us to equip us for the task.'

Such commitment finds its perfect expression in Charles Wesley's hymn:

> Jesus confirm my heart's desire
> to work, and think, and speak for thee;
> still let me guard the holy fire,
> and still stir up thy gift in me.
>
> Ready to do thy perfect will
> my acts of faith and love repeat;

till death thy endless mercies seal,
and make the sacrifice complete.

Mervyn tried to say that hymn daily. And now as that sacrifice is complete his ashes will be scattered at the place he was drawn to time and again at critical moments of his life: Chanctonbury Ring. And those who knew him best can affirm that he sought to serve his King 'with a constant' and most certainly with 'a dangerous and expensive loyalty'.

'Do you think it was worthwhile?' he imagines his cat Midge asking him (in his autobiography) as she lay on the end of that king-sized bed and he replies: 'I hope so. But God's mathematics are different from mine. When he adds up the column of figures on successes and failures, he arrives at a number which is not to be found on a human computer.'

But I am moved to end with some words of Mervyn's: words with which he ended his farewell sermon at Great St Mary's, the church perhaps, together with All Saints, that remained closest to his heart. For those who loved him these words say it all:

I have told you that man is basically a lonely creature. No matter how close his ties may be with other people, much of his life is spent alone, and he knows as little of those he loves best as they know of him. And I think of man's experience of life and of God as a climb up a mountain. For much of the way we go with those who share our lives, but then we come to a point where we must go on alone and climb by ourselves. And it is then on the path on the side of the cliff we shall find ourselves on a narrow ledge. And as we stand there, with so little to support us, the wind rushes past our heads and the Spirit of God speaks: 'Bone of my bone. Flesh of my flesh.'

Francis of Assisi experienced precisely that; and when he came to himself, he found that in his hands and in his feet were the marks of the nails and in his side the thrust of the spear.

'Bone of my bone and flesh of my flesh.' And so we find our consummation and our peace.

7

The Doing of the *Opus Dei*

*The Celebration of the 950th Anniversary of the
Founding of the Abbey Church of St Mary: Sermon
Preached at Festival Eucharist, Coventry Cathedral,
Sunday 12 September 1993*

Words from the Rule of St Benedict, chapter 43:
'Let nothing be preferred to the service of God.'

This weekend many of you are celebrating the 950th anniversary
of the founding of your cathedral just 24 years before Edward
the Confessor built Westminster Abbey. If I feel a shade
fraudulent in this setting, it is because if you ask historians
what the links were between the Benedictines of Westminster
and the Benedictines of Coventry the answer is a resounding
silence. Indeed, the only link I can find between Coventry and
Westminster is in one Richard Neale who, as Dean of Westminster
in 1605, befriended the young George Herbert, then a scholar
at Westminster School. Neale became Bishop of Lichfield and
Coventry in 1610. Neale complained that he had been beaten so
often at Westminster that he never learned any Latin, but that
did not prevent him from playing a dizzy game of preferments
that was all ladders and no snakes. Launching himself from the
Deanery of Westminster, in 22 years he successively became
Bishop of Rochester, Bishop of Lichfield and Coventry, Bishop of
Lincoln, Bishop of Durham, Bishop of Winchester and, finally,
Archbishop of York – not bad going, even by Stuart standards.

In a week that has contained its predictable stories of violence and bloodshed and genocide, a good number of you have come to Coventry to study the monastic life of the Middle Ages. Those who judge that an irrelevance, a form of escapism from the horrors that nightly fill our screens, might have said the same of those who, during the Wars of the Roses or the Black Death, escaped into the relative calm and order of the monastic life. Others of us would claim that those who down the centuries have sought to follow a religious Rule, like that of St Benedict, and live in monastic communities – Eastern or Western, active or contemplative – are like those who seeing a pearl of great price, or a treasure hidden in a field, renounce everything in order to achieve it; and that their way of life could not be more relevant to the values by which we are called to live. For what the best of them have glimpsed and striven for is the Kingdom of God; and what they have attempted, by a life of obedience, humility and prayerful silence, is to show what it means to be a human being created in God's image as well as to demonstrate what a true community under God might be.

The Benedictine Rule, that under the abbot ordered the life of the monasteries of Coventry and Westminster, saw daily life as all of a piece: worship *and* daily work *and* feeding the hungry, clothing the naked and welcoming the stranger were inseparable, and could not be divided into that which is of God and that which is not. Prayer penetrated life, and daily life and work was not so much interrupted by, as contained within and stitched together by, the seven Daily Offices and the daily Mass, from Matins at 2 a.m. to Compline just before sleep: those seven Offices that Cranmer later so brilliantly condensed into our Matins and Evensong. They were the golden thread that bound together this wise and adaptable Rule.

So the monks' chief work was the doing of the *Opus Dei*, the work of God: that is to say, the singing of the divine Offices and the performing of the Eucharist. This is why the great monastic abbeys and churches were built: in order that the worship of God, the singing of the psalms, the reading of the Scriptures and the celebrating of the Eucharist might be done not just with care and devotion, but aided by all the richness of architecture, all the subtlety of colour and ceremonial, all the beauty of words and music, of which we human beings are capable when we approach God – or, rather, when we invite God to approach us.

St Benedict was a man who understood the mystery and complexity of a human being. Like all great spiritual teachers, he recognized the deep sense of incompleteness and yearning within each of us. We have a need for that which transcends us: that which is beyond and other than ourselves and that may come through music or theatre or art or nature; but Christians believe that all these are pointers to the One who is the source of all beauty and truth and in whose likeness we are made. The God who has revealed himself as Christlike and in whom alone lies our true fulfilment.

Now what a great building like yours or mine can do is to take you out of yourself, to arouse in you this sense of awe and wonder; and to feel awe is to begin to worship. Week by week tens of thousands come into the Abbey, thousands come into this cathedral, people of all faiths and none, people who have eyes to see and those who are spiritually blind; and there will be among them many who are hurt and damaged.

My point is simply this: anyone may come at any moment into this space; and through music or architecture or word or liturgy God may touch them, speak to them, take them briefly out of themselves so that they glimpse some spark of truth, or become aware of their own mystery, as they never have before.

Which is why in the end the only reason for the existence of our churches, great or small, is what the Rule of St Benedict calls the *Opus Dei*, the work of God, the daily round of prayer and psalms and canticles and the reading of

Scripture, the daily taking and blessing and breaking and sharing of the eucharistic bread, for all these things speak, in the space that is here and the moment that is now, of the eternal truths of God and our encounter with him in Christ.

That is why for us at Westminster nothing is more important, for example, than the corporate silence with which we start each day; or the singing of Evensong on a weekday evening in winter; or the daily lunchtime Eucharist in the nave with the tourists flowing all around you. All are part of the *Opus Dei*, and everything else we do is secondary to that. And, costly though it sometimes is, it must be done with attentive care.

I can think of many points where this has a direct relevance to the daily evidence of our inhumanity; I offer you just one. Once you dismiss the mystery of each human being made in the divine image; once awe and wonder count for nothing; once our sense of the holy and the transcendent are denied; then life becomes cheap and it becomes possible to shatter with a single bullet those most miraculous objects, the human brain and the human heart, with scarcely a second thought.

By our daily round of prayer and worship, the doing of the *Opus Dei*, we stand with those who affirm night and day that God is worthy of our love and praise, and that every living soul, made in God's likeness, is of infinite value in his sight.

Part 3

Articles and Reviews

8

The Other Side of the Dark

2003

In the spring of 1985, in my mid-fifties, I had spent six happy, busy, spinning years in the parish of Great St Mary's, Cambridge. While wonderfully fulfilling, it was also stressful, not least for a perfectionist. I had a viral illness and my immune system didn't recover. I was left with a total loss of energy, extreme muscle discomfort, swollen glands, aching limbs, a gnawing pain in the lungs, a persistent nausea and an inability to concentrate or remember words. I was to be housebound for a year.

After the first few paralysing weeks I was able (on good days) to walk slowly once round our garden, though it felt like walking through mud. I visited clinic after clinic. All the tests proved negative. One doctor diagnosed toxoplasmosis (wrong); a second, pleurisy (wrong); a third, glandular fever (wrong); eventually they stopped guessing. I tried acupuncture, large doses of vitamins, an octogenarian homeopathic doctor (who, unlike the NHS doctors concerned with malfunctioning bits of my body, encouraged me by looking at me holistically, diminished in body, mind and spirit), but all too soon he died; and the laying-on of hands. I wasn't sure what to try next. I thought of the Emperor Menelik II, the resourceful creator of modern Ethiopia, who was in the habit of nibbling a few pages of the Bible whenever he became ill. In 1913, while recovering from a stroke, he ate the entire book of Kings and died.

But in the end, I was one of the lucky ones. After 18 months

I seemed well enough to take up my new post at Westminster Abbey. Three months later I was struggling again, and only then was I referred to an expert neurologist who named my illness as Myalgic Encephalomyelitis (ME). He explained that it arises from an inappropriate bodily response to a viral illness (often complicated by stress) that results in neurochemical disturbances in the brain and with a profound effect on the immune, endocrine and nervous systems. Psychologically, a diagnosis is a huge relief, and once safely diagnosed I began to improve.

During my long convalescence I had written a short book, *A Year Lost and Found*, in which I tried to describe as honestly as I could what it felt like to be knocked flat in mid-journey and left struggling in the dark. The response took me by storm. After 15 years the book has sold 15,000 copies and is still selling, and I have found it hard to cope with the hundreds of letters that have come as a result and the many people who have wanted to come and talk. After reading it, an elderly priest (with perfect English discretion) asked if I enjoyed undressing in public? To which the answer was 'not much, but sometimes, if you are going to speak in words with which people can identify, and from which hopefully they can take comfort, then you have no other option'. For at that time, many doctors were dismissing their patients' stubbornly persisting symptoms as 'yuppie flu', leaving them not only diminished but demoralized.

Too often we professionals – priests, doctors, counsellors – can allow what we perceive to be the boundaries of our role to inhibit us. Professionalism may properly involve a holding back of large parts of oneself, yet (as Wordsworth wrote) 'we all share one human heart' and there are times when we need to share our stories as a way of affirming our common humanity and helping to authenticate what others may be going through. In one sense it is true that (as a professional) when you sit with someone, listening to their pain and trying to assess their need, you must seek to combine compassion with a necessary professional distance, one foot remaining on the riverbank. No counsellor will be of much help if both are floundering in deep waters; yet people are not problems to be solved, but *mysteries to be loved*, and they may only be drawn to you in the first place if they sense that you too have known at times what it feels like to stumble along in the dark.

Montaigne writes in one of his essays:

> Plato was right in saying that to become a true doctor a man must have experienced all the illnesses he hopes to cure and all the accidents and circumstances he is to diagnose. Such a man I would trust. For the rest guide us like the person who paints seas, rocks and harbours while sitting at his table and sails his model of a ship in perfect safety. Throw him into the real thing, and he does not know where to begin.

An impossible ideal, yet I think we get the point. Only with imagination and empathy can we know at a deep heart-level what it feels like to be bereaved or seriously ill or to be sent spinning by life at its cruelest. And if you have tasted something of the dark shadowlands of sickness or pain or loss that most people enter at some point in their lives, then it will deepen your compassion. People who come in search of help and healing seem to recognize intuitively a kindred spirit: someone who knows the feel of that landscape; someone who knows, too, that there is light on the other side of the dark. By knowing when to hide and when to share our vulnerability we can affirm one another on the often-distressing human journey.

But life has moved on. My then unfashionable illness is now known as ME/CFS (Chronic Fatigue Syndrome), though not all neurologists lump the two together quite so neatly; and 'fatigue' carries the suggestion that you are permanently tired when you are not so much tired as totally weak, daily drained of energy. It has at last been officially diagnosed by the Government Chief Medical Officer's Report (2002) as a severe and potentially disabling clinically diagnosed condition affecting four people in every thousand, people of all ages (and recognized, incidentally, as the single most common cause of absence from school). It most commonly affects highly capable and very active people, and a full and complete recovery becomes less likely for adults who have the full flush of medically agreed symptoms for more than four years. Of course such generalizations are unhelpful, for each person's illness and projected recovery is unique to them. And even in the most severe cases there may be quite long periods of remission, that larger pattern replicating the depressingly unpredictable pattern of the initial illness, where you may seem to be making progress, only to find yourself (often for no apparent reason) back where you started. For many it is a frustrating switchback of minor peaks and troughs, an undulating graph, though if you are sensible, patient, hopeful (and, no doubt, fortunate) the line of the graph will in time return to normal.

My life, too, has moved on; there have been three other books, somewhat more ambitious and diverse; yet (infuriatingly!) it's the ME book that people most often write about; and looking back, I realize that this illness, which at the time seemed so devastating, was paradoxically one of the most fruitful things that happened to me. For *A Year Lost and Found* was not only about the vulnerability we all share, it was also about the sort of questions I urgently needed to ask myself if the experience was not to be wasted and for something creative, and therefore redemptive, to emerge from what felt like a wholly negative period of my life and ministry.

So what did my time of sickness teach me? Not much that I did not know, but the difference was that I came to understand certain truths at a far more profound level, a shift from mind to heart.

1 The need for inner space

I had asked my homeopathic doctor why my immune system had failed to respond, why I had proved so vulnerable? 'Perhaps,' he said with a smile, 'because your inscape does not match your landscape. You have all the stiffness,' he added, 'of the public man.' He was telling me that those truths I sought to live by, the inner landscape of my heart, didn't really match that world where I had to function as an over-busy professional with a circumscribed role seeking (and failing) to meet all kinds of ill-defined expectations. He helped restore my sense of worth. Over the months I was forced to reconsider my priorities and, above all, the lack of that inner space born of simple daily contemplation that restores the balance in an overactive life, and that people have a right to look for in their clergy.

2 The need for positive thinking

I understood the isolation that illness brings. 'As sickness is the greatest mystery,' wrote John Donne, 'so the great misery of illness is solitude.' When you are ill your world is reduced to your aches and pains, and you become anxious, and perhaps angry and, in the small hours of the night, full of self-pity. Illness means a fundamental change to the way in which you perceive and experience your body. You are forced to acknowledge your impotence and your mortality. Indeed, it has been said, 'Disease can so alter the relationship that the body is no longer seen as a friend but rather, as an untrustworthy enemy', and as the illness continues you feel increasingly vulnerable. A vital part of that healing is the reversal of this negative, self-absorbed way of thinking. I learned that my illness was uniquely mine, a subjective experience, an inner event that can't be fully shared even with the one who loves you most. But I wanted people to try. Our illnesses and our reaction to them are as individual as our faces or our fingerprints. My illness was an expression of the unique and vulnerable person I was, not simply a clinical case with a textbook diagnosis. For a short while I was lucky enough to find a doctor who understood that each of us is an interrelated whole, an embodied spirit, and who went beyond the clinical questions to ask those deeper questions: 'What is it like for you?' It has been estimated that 70 per cent of all medical care is 'good mothering' and 70 per cent of the healing process performed by healing powers and resources the patient already possesses.

3 Learning to depend on others

The third lesson I learned was a new dependence on others. When I was diminished physically and mentally, I was equally diminished spiritually. While I rediscovered the power of the psalms to speak to every aspect of our human journey, I found it almost impossible to pray. Yet somehow that didn't matter, for I knew that I was wonderfully upheld and supported by others, and that morning and evening I was being named at the Eucharist and at Evening Prayer. Visitors who were brief, affirming and tactile (and who weren't tempted to talk about their own past illnesses) were very welcome – especially those who understood the cost of a drawn-out, seemingly unchanging illness to those who care for you.

4 Discovering the God who is vulnerable

My illness (so trivial compared to the darkness so many face) confirmed a truth that lies at the heart of the mystery that is suffering: the fact that life is unpredictable and frequently unfair, too often claiming the good and the innocent among its victims, but that God does not intervene either to answer our bewildered questions or to play tricks with our freedom; instead he does that more astonishing thing: *he enters with us into the questions.* Calvary is a window into the bewildering truth of the Christlike God who suffers within and alongside his creatures, and is, as we are, vulnerable to pain. But that is another story for another time.

5 Everything may be redeemed

But the last lesson I learned was that my long year of illness was not simply *lost* but also *found.* The theme of death and resurrection that runs like a golden thread through creation and through our human story is an affirmation that nothing need ever be wasted, that good may be brought out of evil, that everything may be redeemed. At my lowest a nun had suggested that I ask myself the question: 'What do I *really* want?'and I had glibly answered: 'To be made well.' But I gradually understood that this was an inadequate answer, for what I really wanted was to know that the year had not been wasted, to learn the lessons of my sickness, to accept that I wanted a different kind of healing. I wanted it to be a valued part of my journey. Perhaps at last I was beginning to glimpse what the apparently absent, always reticent God had been doing all the time.

9

Review of *Embracing the Chaos:Theological Responses to AIDS* edited by James Woodward

At the heart of this book of essays there is a paradox. The institutional Church has failed to respond to those affected by HIV/AIDS with understanding, compassion or hope. The heard message (with certain honourable exceptions) has been either a judgemental and fearful condemnation, or a thunderous silence. Yet the Church of the incarnation places a high value on the flesh, centres on a death, speaks of a vulnerable God who comes alongside us in our suffering and redefines the nature of loving relationships within communities. Churches should be places where people may share their vulnerability and find healing, places of openness and love; and those of us who have been privileged to witness the AIDS support groups that have burgeoned in our larger cities cannot but be moved by (and made ashamed by) the supportive love, forgiveness and acceptance that are often found there.

Theology is a way of exploring life in the light of our faith in God, of facing death in the light of Easter, and of interpreting our most painful experiences in the light of the cross and its power to redeem tragedy and despair; yet there has been little attempt to face the theological, moral or pastoral issues raised by AIDS. As Edward Norman points out in his outstanding essay, the appearance of AIDS gives the Churches an opportunity 'to re-examine their theology of human sexuality ... and to ask whether homosexual orientation and conduct should be revalued' in the light of the reinterpretation of its moral and disciplinary teachings that the Church must undertake in every age.

James Woodward has coordinated much richness in a short space. Peter Baelz on the nature of God and the nature of the world is admirable – as is his warning to recognize the moral choices we must make, once we know God accepts us as we are, if we are to become what we have it in us to be. Kenneth Leech gives us heady stuff on 'the material and carnal character of grace and of the spirit', and has hard things to say about our loss of passion.

Interspersed with the essays are painful, often bitterly honest, responses to AIDS and the Church from those who have died or who are living with HIV; an uncomfortable earthing of the surrounding theologians – though, to their credit, all the contributors speak with a rare realism and humanity.

Michael Mayne
Westminster Abbey

10

Review of *The Stranger in the Wings*: *Affirming Faith in a God of Surprises* by Richard Holloway

Critics ought to be unbiased, which I am not. I opened Richard Holloway's latest book with an anticipatory sense of wonder and gratitude. Wonder that the Primus of the Scottish Episcopal Church can be so prolific – 16 books in 22 years, yet only marginally repetitive – and gratitude that time and again, when asked by people for a humane and popular communicator of Christian truth, I have confidently suggested Richard Holloway.

The Stranger in the Wings is about whether Christianity is a protectionist sect, trapped in an unchanging and unchangeable past, or a trusting, risk-taking way of being open to the new. If our theology, our God-talk, is dynamic; if Easter is about letting go of the God of the past and discovering the God of the present (and the future); if the work of the Spirit is to continue to open our eyes; then the tradition we inherit is a living reality, not a game of 'pass the parcel in which the Church hands on a pre-packed body of truth'.

That the Christlike, self-emptying God comes to us and that we find him in unexpected places is asserted in Part I of the book; Part II explores these truths in those areas where 'the stranger in the wings' has spoken to Holloway most powerfully: among the homeless, the marginalized of El Salvador, and those affected by the AIDS virus. He is particularly good on the nature of truth (which is 'the result of conflict and collision, and is never absolute'); the necessary tension of a properly inclusive Anglicanism; and the relation of the Church and Kingdom. He is as sharply critical of 'Little Englanders' as of fundamentalists.

Part of the Afterword on 'dust and glory' is a kind of Holloway purple patch that he has used before, word for word. It left me with a pang of guilt. I began quoting it years ago, and have repeated it so often that I had come to think of the words as my own. Which is meant, not so much as an apology, but as a tribute to a writer of rare and enviable perception.

Michael Mayne
Westminster Abbey

Acknowledgements of Sources

'On a Huge Hill' was first published in *Tradition and Unity: Sermons in Honour of Robert Runcie*, edited by Dan Cohn-Sherbok (Bellew, 1991). Permission sought.

'The Doing of the *Opus Dei*' (copyright Michael Mayne) was first published in *Coventry's First Cathedral: The Cathedral and Priory of St Mary. Papers from the 1993 Anniversary Symposium*, edited by George Demidowicz (Paul Watkins of Stamford, 1994).

'The Other Side of the Dark' was first published in *Chrism* (2003), and is published with permission from The Guild of Health and St Raphael. Their website can be found at www.gohealth.org.uk.

Reviews of *Embracing the Chaos: Theological Responses to AIDS*, first published in *Theology* 93 (September/October 1990), and *The Stranger in the Wings: Affirming Faith in a God of Surprises*, first published in *Theology* 98 (May/June 1995) are published with permission from SPCK.

Other published sources
On page 27: T. S. Eliot, 'Choruses from the Rock', *Collected Poems 1909-62* (Faber & Faber, 2002).

On page 30: Peter Shaffer, *Amadeus*, Penguin Classics, 2007.

Index of Names